W9-CLC-116

FOUNDATIONS OF
BIBLICAL FAITH

BIRDVILLE
BAPTIST CHURCH
LIBRARY

FOUNDATIONS OF BIBLICAL FAITH

James T. Draper, Jr.

BIRDVILLE
BAPTIST CHURCH
LIBRARY

BROADMAN PRESS
Nashville, Tennessee

© Copyright 1979 • Broadman Press.

All rights reserved.

4219–51

ISBN: 0–8054–1951–9

Dewey Decimal Classification: 230

Subject heading: THEOLOGY, DOCTRINAL

Library of Congress Catalog Card Number: 78–67001

Printed in the United States of America

To
every Southern Baptist
who stands firm upon the Word of God
as our rule of faith and practice
and who believes
that what we believe about doctrine
does make a difference

BIRDVILLE
BAPTIST CHURCH
LIBRARY

Unless otherwise noted, all Scripture quotations are taken from the King James Version of the Bible.

Scripture quotations marked TLB are taken from *The Living Bible*. Copyright © Tyndale House Publishers, Wheaton, Illinois, 1971. Used by permission.

Scripture quotations marked TEV are taken from *The Bible in Today's English Version*. Old Testament: Copyright © American Bible Society 1976. New Testament: Copyright © American Bible Society 1966, 1971, 1976. Used by permission.

Preface

The following pages were born out of a desire to have a simple, clear discussion of biblical doctrine. I have not been able to find a concise and clearly defined book that is available for the general Christian community. This is not a profound theological treatment of any of the topics contained in these pages. The intent is to briefly present some of the basic doctrines of our Christian faith from a thoroughly conservative view.

It is written from the perspective of one who totally accepts the inerrancy of the Scriptures and believes that God's Word is the final authority for our faith and doctrine. I have written these pages in full understanding that they are woefully inadequate, yet with the earnest prayer that God will use the book as a springboard to deeper study of his Word and of the eternal doctrines of our faith. Every chapter is incomplete. Volumes have been written about each subject.

My prayer is that these pages will help to keep our lives in line with proper doctrine. What we believe does make a difference. Our behavior is based upon our doctrine. False doctrine soon corrupts our lives and leads to excesses of every sort. Compromise is the result of faulty convictions regarding doctrine. These chapters are biblically centered and based upon the deep conviction that what God has said in his Word is valid and is the final word for our belief.

Contents

1
The Revelation of God

It is important for us to begin with a study of God. If we do not have the true concept of God, then we will have wrong concepts about sin, salvation, service, and many other very significant truths. The Bible begins with the assumption of God. The very first verse in the Bible says, "In the beginning God created . . . ." And then the story of God begins. That story is traced throughout the entire Word of God.

When we look at the world and see all of the different ideas about God, we long to know the truth. We want to discover what is right about God. One thing is very evident. We never will know God unless God reveals himself.

Natural Revelation

First note the natural revelation of God. "The invisible things of him from the creation of the world are clearly seen, being understood by the things that are made, even his eternal power and Godhead; so that they are without excuse" (Rom. 1:20). Speaking of those who had not heard the gospel preached, the apostle Paul declared that there is a natural revelation of God in our world. God has revealed himself.

First, there is the revelation we find in material substance. Everything begun owes its existence to some producing cause. We know that we are in a world that has been begun somewhere because things are born; they grow old; and they die. There is no one who would deny the age/cycle factor in the world. Everything as we understand it has a beginning. The very idea that something had a beginning means that it owes its existence to some producing cause. God speaks to us through the material universe. "The heavens declare the glory of God; and the firmament sheweth his handiwork" (Ps. 19:1). This material universe is part of the natural revelation.

A second aspect of the natural revelation is that we have a world of order and purpose. This world may seem irrational, but it is not erratic. It is a world that is governed by certain great natural laws. It would be foolish for us to assume that a world could be governed by laws if there were not a lawgiver or a force behind the laws. Why do the planets not collide and destroy the universe? Food, shelter, and all the things that we need are provided by natural laws. The laws, the order, the purposefulness of this universe require that we have an intelligence adequate to produce it. This is a world of intricate order. We can send a man to the moon because we are aware of the laws that govern the universe. Those laws presuppose an intelligence that would produce such order.

Another part of the natural revelation is the intelligence of man. Man is a rational, moral, and intelligent being. It is inconceivable that intelligence could come out of unintelligence. Assuming that man with his intelligence, his morality, and his rational being just happened is just as ridiculous as explaining the Encyclopaedia Britannica by an explosion at the print shop! The natural revelation of God reveals that the intelligence of man owes its existence to something.

Let's take it a step further. We are capable of looking at

this world and conceiving of a perfect God. And yet perfection demands existence. One could not be perfect if he did not exist. The very idea that the human mind with its intelligence can project a perfect being indicates that such an absolutely perfect being exists.

Another aspect of natural revelation is the religious nature of man. We have never discovered any tribe of people, no matter how primitive, who did not have some form of worship. They will worship something. They will worship the tree. They will worship the sun. They will worship the snake, the fish, the alligator, the lion, the tiger, the elephant, the cattle. They will worship something! If God was just a figment of our imagination, why is belief in God universal with people who have never communicated with each other? The religious nature of man is strong evidence for the existence of God.

Natural revelation can prove the existence of a very powerful God. It cannot prove that the God of the Bible exists, but it gives every evidence of a powerful God. The natural man cannot perceive the things of God because he is not spiritually discerning (1 Cor. 2:14). He has no ability to think in those terms. Though there are strong reasons and great logic for a belief in a very powerful God, natural revelation by itself cannot, beyond question, prove the existence of the God of the Bible. Rather, natural revelation is the foundation for a higher revelation. The reason is obvious.

Nature cannot tell me about love. It cannot tell me how much God cares about me and how much he longs to forgive my sins. Nature cannot tell me about eternity and the life beyond. It does not speak of the future of the human soul and of the kingdom of God. Nature can give me hints and evidences of God, but it cannot tell me what kind of God he is. It cannot tell me what he does for me or his interest in me. Natural revelation, as strong as it is, is only the basis of a greater, more supernatural revelation.

Biblical Revelation

If I am to know God, God must reveal himself to me. The prophet Isaiah declared, "Verily thou art a God that hidest thyself, O God of Israel, the Saviour" (Isa. 45:15). The apostle Paul cried out, "O the depth of the riches both of the wisdom and knowledge of God! how unsearchable are his judgments, and his ways past finding out!" (Rom. 11:33). The Word of God is God's revelation to us. The psalmist pronounced, "The word of the Lord is right; and all his works are done in truth. He loveth righteousness and judgment: the earth is full of the goodness of the Lord. By the word of the Lord were the heavens made; and all the host of them by the breath of his mouth. He gathereth the waters of the sea together as an heap: he layeth up the depth in storehouses. Let all the earth fear the Lord: let all the inhabitants of the world stand in awe of him. For he spake, and it was done; he commanded, and it stood fast" (Ps. 33: 4–9).

To learn about God and his world, we must turn to the Word of God. Paul in writing to Timothy said, "All scripture is given by inspiration of God, and it is profitable for doctrine, for reproof, for correction, for instruction in righteousness: That the man of God may be perfect, thoroughly furnished unto all good works" (2 Tim. 3:16–17). The biblical revelation must be placed side by side with the natural revelation.

First of all, the Bible assumes the existence of God; it does not try to prove God. The Bible writers had a very simple philosophy: Why endeavor to prove the obvious? It would make no sense to try to prove that the sun existed.

That would be rather foolish. All we would need to do is open the window and let the sunshine in. The biblical writers felt no obligation to prove the existence of God. To them, God was a living, vital reality. Thus, there is no attempt in the Scriptures to prove that God exists.

The Bible pictures God as the Creator from the very first chapter in the first book: "In the beginning, God created the heaven and the earth" (Gen. 1:1). In Isaiah 45:12 God declares, "I have made the earth, and created man upon it: I, even my hands, have stretched out the heavens, and all their hosts have I commanded." God is viewed throughout the Word of God as the Creator. This world is not simply something that happened through a cataclysmic collision of forces in nature. It is the result of the guiding, creating, purposeful hand of God.

The Bible further pictures God as the Lord of the universe. Isaiah continued, "I have raised him up in righteousness, and I will direct all his ways: he shall build my city, and he shall let go my captives, not for price nor reward, saith the Lord of hosts. Thus saith the Lord, the labour of Egypt, and merchandise of Ethiopia and of the Sabeans, men of stature, shall come over unto thee, and they shall be thine: they shall come after thee; in chains they shall come over, and they shall fall down unto thee, they shall make supplication unto thee, saying, Surely God is in thee; and there is none else, there is no God. Verily thou art a God that hidest thyself, O God of Israel, the Saviour" (Isa. 45:13–15).

Everywhere the Bible speaks of God as the Lord of the universe. Exodus 15 calls God one who is greater than all gods. Deuteronomy 10 calls him "God of Gods, and Lord of Lords" (v. 17). First Chronicles 16 declares he is to be "feared above all gods" (v. 25). Psalm 95 reveals him as the "great King above all gods" (v. 3). The Bible pictures

God as the moving, ruling force in the universe.

The Bible portrays God as the sustainer of life. In the first chapter of Genesis we read that God turned to Adam and Eve and said, "Be fruitful, and multiply, and replenish the earth, and subdue it" (Gen. 1:28). Then God said, "Behold, I have given you every herb bearing seed, which is upon the face of all the earth, and every tree, in the which is the fruit of a tree yielding seed; to you it shall be meat. And to every beast of the earth, and to every fowl of the air, and to every thing that creepeth upon the earth, wherein there is life, I have given every green herb for meat: and it was so. And God saw every thing that he had made, and, behold, it was very good" (Gen. 1:29–31).

God provided for them everything they needed. God was not only their Creator; he was their sustainer. He told them how to eat and how to live. The apostle Paul, as he stood on Mars' Hill in Athens, said, "In him we live, and move, and have our being" (Acts 17:28). He is everything.

More than that, the Bible pictures God as the Redeemer. He is the one who loves us and who provides for every spiritual and physical need we have. Early in the Bible God promises to send the Messiah, who will come to save the people from their sins (Gen. 3:15–21). God is our Redeemer.

Personal Revelation

Look at the personal revelation. God has revealed himself through the Bible, but he is still revealing himself to us. Being saved is not simply saying that certain things are true and accepting certain doctrine as being correct. Being saved is knowing God. There is a personal revelation of God in our world. Notice Job's answer to God. "I know that thou canst do every thing, and that no thought can be withholden from thee. Who is he that hideth counsel without knowl-

edge? therefore have I uttered that I understand not . . .
Here, I beseech thee, and I will speak: I will demand of
thee, and declare thou unto me" (Job 42:2–4). He was saying
that there were many things he knew about God and many
things he did not understand.

Now notice verse 5: "I have heard of thee by the hearing
of the ear: but now mine eye seeth thee." Once he had
simply heard of God but now he has experienced his
presence.

When Isaiah was confronted by his call to be a prophet,
he cried out, "Woe is me! for I am undone; because I am
a man of unclean lips, and I dwell in the midst of a people
of unclean lips: for mine eyes have seen the King, the Lord
of hosts. I heard the voice of the Lord, saying, Whom shall
I send, and who will go for us? Then said I, Here am I;
send me" (Isa. 6:5,8).

God had become very personal to Isaiah. God was no
longer just an abstract concept. God was no longer simply
a great moving force in the universe. God was now a personal
God to him. There is a natural revelation of God and there
is a biblical revelation of God, but there is a personal revelation of God in our hearts and lives.

God will reveal himself to us personally. When we are
saved, Jesus Christ plants his life in us through his Holy
Spirit. Paul exclaimed, "I am crucified with Christ: nevertheless I live; yet not I, but Christ liveth in me" (Gal. 2:20).
Salvation is letting God become our God. There are many
people who have spent their lives in churches but have never
had a personal revelation of God. They see the natural revelation of God and they hear biblical revelation of God, but
somehow God has never come alive to them. If we will
receive him into our hearts, God will reveal himself to us
personally.

More than that, God will forgive our sins. The guilt that drives us, the sin that hounds and haunts us, will be cleansed and forgiven. That is what he longs to do. When he reveals himself personally to us, he will forgive our sins. "If we walk in the light, as he is in the light, we have fellowship one with another, and the blood of Jesus Christ his Son cleanseth us from all sin" (1 John 1:7). When God reveals himself to us personally, he will forgive our sins and give us new life. He will control our temper. He will transform our evil tendencies. "If any man be in Christ, he is a new creature: old things are passed away; behold, all things are become new" (2 Cor. 5:17). That is the personal revelation of God.

Now consider the most vital truth concerning the revelation of God. We cannot understand the natural revelation of God or the personal revelation of God without the biblical revelation. The biblical revelation explains it to us. We cannot understand what is happening unless we see it in the light of God's revealed Word. If we do not understand nature in the light of God's Word, then we will see the storms and the tornadoes that destroy life and property and conclude that God is an angry God who destroys and delights in depriving people of that which is precious to them. When the sun bakes the earth and the drought keeps the rain away and the crops dry up, we will view God as a God who teases and keeps his people from having the provision they need. We will not understand these experiences without the Bible.

We are on very dangerous ground to take experience as ultimate truth. If we interpret God by our experience, we are accepting a philosophical concept of God and not a biblical concept of God. Experience is not the determining factor. We conclude that if we tingle, that must be God; if we weep, that must be God; if we speak in other languages, that must be God. God may do all those things, but those things do not necessarily mean God is doing them. I have known people to get excited and be deliriously happy and never be saved. There are at least five pagan religions that speak in tongues, and they do not even claim the name of Jesus Christ.

If we do not measure our experience and natural revelation by the Bible, we will never know God as he really is. We see God about us in every evidence of nature. We experience wonderful blessings and wonderful gifts of God, but we bring them all in line with and interpret them all in the light of the Word of God.

Most of us would not claim to be atheists, but many of us are practical atheists. The dogmatic atheist declares, "There is no God," and he is guilty of infidelity to God. The practical atheist believes there is a God, but lives as if there were none. He is guilty of impiety. Do not claim to believe in God and then live as if God were dead or did not exist. In Psalm 14:1 we read, "The fool hath said in his heart, There is not God." The fool is the one who says, "There is a God, but I wish that he didn't exist; I wish it were not so." He shakes his fist in the face of God and pushes him aside. Many believe in God but practice atheism.

If there is a God who has revealed himself through nature, through the Bible, and through personal experience, and we live as if he does not exist, then we are guilty of the greatest possible blasphemy.

2
The Character of God

It is one thing to talk about the existence of God; but when we try to describe God in just a few pages, frustration is a natural end result. God took great pains to write an entire book about himself. There are so many references, so many things we could say. Thus, I admit to my frustration. This will be a very incomplete chapter.

The revelation of God is *that* God is, but the character of God is *what* God is. "I would seek unto God, and unto God would I commit my cause: Which doeth great things and unsearchable; marvellous things without number" (Job 5:8–9). Unsearchable and marvelous without number are the deeds of God. We cannot count them.

"Who giveth rain upon the earth, and sendeth waters upon the fields: To set up on high those that be low; that those which mourn may be exalted to safety. He disappointeth the devices of the crafty, so that their hands cannot perform their enterprise. He taketh the wise in their own craftiness: and the counsel of the forward is carried headlong. They meet with darkness in the daytime, and grope in the noonday as in the night. But he saveth the poor from the sword, from their mouth, and from the hand of the mighty. So the poor hath hope, and iniquity stoppeth her mouth. Behold, happy is the man whom God correcteth: therefore despise not thou the chastening of the Almighty: For he maketh sore, and bindeth up: he woundeth, and his hands make whole" (Job 5:10–18).

There are many false ideas about God. To some people, God is only an impersonal great, first cause of the universe. They readily acknowledge the existence of God but have no awareness of the reality of a God who can be known. There are other people to whom God is a doting old grandfather. They think that if they promise him something, he will do anything they want him to do. They consider him to be an old fool who will let them get away with almost anything. That is the way most folks live. To other people, God is a tyrant. He delights in restricting, hindering, and making us unhappy. To these people everything about God is negative. When we consider the kind of God who is revealed in the Bible and the way most people treat him, we realize that many view God in an inadequate way.

What is God really like? What does the Bible say to us about the nature and the character of God? There are four statements for us to consider concerning the character of God.

God Is Spirit

The most elementary truth of the Bible is that God is spirit. That in itself staggers our imagination. We cannot imagine a spirit. We cannot imagine a formless mind or a formless being. Yet the Bible clearly tells us that God is a spirit. Jesus, in talking to the woman at the well, declared, "God is a Spirit: and they that worship him must worship him in spirit and in truth" (John 4:24). The psalmist extolled, "Great is our Lord, and of great power: his understanding is infinite" (Ps. 147:5).

God is a spiritual being. Spirit is the highest form of being. It is infinite, without limitation. Everything material is lim-

ited by space and by time. But God is not confined to the
limitations of matter or of space. He has no body, so he is
not bound by gravity, disease, or death. He is limitless in
his being. He is pure in quality. He is immeasurably superior
to anything else. The word *infinite* speaks of the spirituality
of God. Since he is Spirit, there are some characteristics
that are his alone.

God Is a Person

God is a person with intelligence. He is a person who
thinks and acts. He is a person to whom we can respond.
He has a personality. This is demonstrated by the fact that
he gives himself a name. When Moses asked the name of
God, God replied, "I AM THAT I AM . . . . Thus shalt thou
say unto the children of Israel, I AM hath sent me unto
you" (Ex. 3:14). He is a person of self-knowledge, of self-
understanding. He is a person who has identified himself
for us and thus indicates that he is a person of intelligence.

He is the living God, the everlasting God. "In him was
life; and the life was the light of men" (John 1:4). He is
Spirit and an intelligent person with life. This is more than
we can imagine. That is why Jesus Christ came. God sent
Jesus Christ so we would know what God himself is like.
We can all identify with the little black boy who said, "I
want a God what's got skin on." We want a God we can
see.

We also want a God we can touch. Jesus Christ is God's
self-revelation to us. Jesus Christ is God in the flesh. In Jesus
Christ, God came in physical form so that we could see and
know him. This God who is a Spirit has revealed himself
in Jesus Christ.

Since Jesus Christ has returned to heaven, where does

God live? He lives in us. Just as Jesus was God in the flesh, so the Spirit of God desires to find residence in us. This infinite God, this Spirit God, this intelligent, life-giving, life-supplying God can come and dwell in us. He came in the form of man in Jesus Christ. He multiplies himself through us. Jesus said, "The works that I do . . . greater works than these shall he do" (John 14:12).

None of us has ever done a greater thing than Jesus did when he died on the cross. We have never achieved a greater thing than Jesus did when he led captivity captive and led those out of paradise into the glory of himself. How can we do greater things than he did? We will do greater things because there will be more of us now, and God will be revealing and working through more than just one person. He was working through Jesus Christ, a person we can see. When Jesus went away he sent his Spirit; and it is the purpose of this Spirit-God, this intelligent, life-giving God, to indwell us and to fill us. Thus, instead of one body working the miracles of God's grace through God's Spirit and power, now he possesses millions of bodies. Through each one of them God reveals himself to a lost world. Thus we do greater things than Christ.

God Is Infinite

There is a third statement concerning God: God is infinite. We are finite; God is infinite. We are limited; God is not limited. There are several concepts that are included in the idea of an infinite God. One concept is *omnipotence.* If God is infinite, he is omnipotent. *Omni* means all and *potent* means power, so he is all-powerful. Job declared, "I know that thou canst do every thing and that no thought can be withholden from thee" (Job 42:2). Remember the beautiful

statement made by Jesus, "With men this is impossible; but
with God all things are possible" (Matt. 19:26). God can do
anything he wills to do.

Sometimes we think that omnipotence means that God
can do anything. When we think that is all that it means,
we miss the real meaning. God cannot lie, so that means
he cannot do everything. God cannot deny himself; he cannot sin; he cannot act contrary to his own being. There is
a sense in which God cannot do everything. We can better
understand omnipotence if we realize that God can do anything he wills to do. God can do anything consistent with
his nature. God can do anything consistent with his love
and with his mercy, with what he is and who he is. He is
an omnipotent God. Anything he wills, he can do.

There is another *omni*. He is *omnipresent*. That is, he is
all-present. We can better understand this if we do not think
of God as being everywhere but as being everywhere man
is. God is forever interested in us as individuals. We best
understand the omnipresence of God if we realize that wherever we go, God is there. Rather than God just being in
some void, just existing, he is relating to man.

The psalmist said, "Whither shall I go from thy spirit?
or whither shall I flee from thy presence? If I ascend up
into heaven, thou art there: if I make my bed in hell, behold,
thou art there. If I take the wings of the morning, and dwell
in the uttermost parts of the sea; Even there shall thy hand
lead me, and thy right hand shall hold me" (Ps. 139:7–10).
God is forever relating himself to us, identifying himself
with us. He is omnipresent. Jacob said, "Surely the Lord is
in this place; and I knew it not. And he was afraid, and
said, How dreadful is this place! this is none other but the
house of God, and this is the gate of heaven" (Gen. 28:16,17).

Wherever we are, God is. If we will come to understand

this meaning of the omnipresence of God, how we live will make a difference. It would make a difference how children talked to their parents if they realized God was present. It would make a difference in discussions at home if we recognized the presence of God. When we come to the understanding that God is always there, that God sees all we do and is aware of all we think, this greatly affects our lives. Though we may be alone in the sense of not being with other people, God is wherever we are. We must forever live in that awareness.

We now speak of the *omniscience* of God, the wisdom of God. He understands all knowledge, all wisdom. The omniscience of God does not simply mean that he knows all the facts. It means that he uses knowledge properly. God never makes any mistakes. He never makes a wrong move. In speaking of the wisdom of God, the psalmist said, "O Lord, thou hast searched me, and known me. Thou knowest my downsitting and mine uprising, thou understandest my thought afar off. Thou compassest my path and my lying down, and art acquainted with all my ways. For there is not a word in my tongue, but, lo, O Lord, thou knowest it altogether. Thou has beset me behind and before, and laid thine hand upon me. Such knowledge is too wonderful for me; it is high, I cannot attain unto it" (Ps. 139:1–6). God is perfect knowledge, wisdom, and understanding. He is omniscient. He is a wise and gracious God.

He is *eternal.* The word of God indicates that he is the everlasting God. Genesis 21:33; Psalm 90:2; 100:5, and literally hundreds of verses deal with the everlasting nature of God. He never had a beginning and will never have an ending. He never started and will never stop. He is an eternal God, an everlasting God. That may astonish us. But can we imagine a God who is not like that? He would not be

God if he did not have those qualities. He would be less
than God if he did not have perfection in every way. Perfection speaks of perfect existence, and a perfect existence
would be an eternal existence. God is infinite, and that also
means that he is eternal.

God Is Absolute

There is one other statement to make concerning God.
God is *absolute*. Several things are involved in that. One
is *immutability*. That means he does not change. Hebrews
1:11; 1 Samuel 15:29; Isaiah 14:24; 46:9–10 speak of the stead-
fast purposes of God. God's purposes never change. God's
actions may vary depending upon our response to God, but
his purposes are always the same. Jesus Christ is the same
yesterday, today, and forever (Heb. 13:8). God is a consistent
God. His purposes, his desires, his plans never change. His
basic underlying purpose for us relates to us individually
and uniquely, but it never changes. There is a unity about
God. There are no divisions in God. There are no conflicts
in God's being. Early in the Old Testament, God declared
that he is one God. There is a unity of being, of existence,
and of relationship.

More than that, God is *holy* (Ex. 15:11). Concerning God,
Peter said, "Be ye holy; for I am holy" (1 Pet. 1:16).

There are three things that relate to the holiness of God.
First, holy means *separate*. God is different. There is a sepa-
rateness about God. When Isaiah became aware of the presence of God, he realized he was in the presence of someone
different than he. There is a uniqueness about God, a purity
about God. Holiness means that God is not like us. We are
sinful; God is righteous and holy. Holy means separate.

Holiness also carries with it the idea of *condemnation*.
When Isaiah realized how holy God was, he cried, "O, how

unholy I am." One thing the holiness of God does is condemn our unholiness, our sinfulness. When we stand in the presence of a holy God, we are made aware that we are sinners. There is the aspect of condemnation in the holiness of God.

There is the element of *mercy* also. God is holy. His holiness condemns me, but his holiness also reaches out in mercy for me. Forgiveness is a radiant certainty for our lives. Forgiveness is God's design and desire. It was in God's heart that the redemptive purposes for mankind were born. God's holiness demanded satisfaction, and God stepped in to provide that satisfaction and make it possible for us to be forgiven. The psalmist frequently talks about this mercy. "Thy mercy is great unto the heavens, and thy truth unto the clouds. Be thou exalted, O God, above the heavens; let thy glory be above all the earth" (Ps. 57:10–11). The holiness of God means that he is separate from us. We stand condemned, and yet we are reached by the mercy of God which is a part of his holiness.

God is a God of *righteousness*. God will always deal fairly. His righteousness is absolute. "He is the Rock, his work is perfect: for all his ways are judgment; a God of truth and without iniquity, just and right is he" (Deut. 32:4). God's righteousness is a perfect kind of righteousness.

God is also *perfect truth*. If we want to know truth, we will never discover it until we discover it in God. There is no ultimate truth apart from God. Truth is simply fact that degenerates into incomprehension unless we know God, who is the truth. Jesus said, "I am the way, the truth, and the life" (John 14:6).

There are many things to know about God. He is Spirit. He is a person. He is infinite. He is absolute. That is more than we can comprehend or imagine. The attributes of God stagger our minds. But one thing we know: God never mag-

nifies one of his attributes at the expense of another. God
never contradicts himself. Mercy and justice are not incom-
patible. Doing what is right and, at the same time, being
compassionate, loving, and merciful is not contradictory.

His infinite and absolute nature tells us that God is sovereign. God can do what he chooses. He is in control. Yet
his sovereignty does not violate my free will. My free will
is the result of one of God's characteristics, for he is a self-
limiting God. He is a God of infinite wisdom. His wisdom
means that he has the ability to use knowledge rightly so
that he does not make mistakes. God has limited himself
so that while he is sovereign, we are free. We cannot understand that. But this much we may know: God's attributes
are not contradictory. God does not contradict himself.
Righteousness and peace are in complete harmony.

God has given to us the ability and the desire to respond
to him. God is a Spirit; yet that Spirit became flesh and
dwelt among us and revealed what he is like. That God
exists is unquestionable. Through Jesus Christ and through
his word we find the revelation of what God is like. How
are we to know God? We know him through his word—
the living word and the written Word. Jesus said, "No man
cometh unto the Father, but by me" (John 14:6). Jesus is
the embodiment of God. Jesus is the physical expression
of God. No man can know God except he knows him through
Jesus Christ. He may know about God, but he cannot know
God except through Jesus Christ.

Now, how are we to know about Jesus Christ? Through
his Word! We do not know about Jesus Christ by our experience. That is too subjective. We know him by his Word.
That is how we keep things straight. We avoid concepts of
God that are wrong by staying with what God has said. We
do not change it; we apply it. We know God through his

Word. We know about Jesus through his Word.

We look in a telescope and see the immensity of space. It staggers our minds to think of the billions of celestial bodies. And to think that he is the God of all that. It is staggering! Yet one atom, which is smaller than we can see with the average microscope, is only one small part of matter. There are forty thousand atoms in one molecule. The God of infinite, staggering space is also the God of minute detail. The God of the immensity of space can narrow himself down and live in me. Our God is big enough to make a home in our lives. The important thing is not just that God *is* but that God *is in me*.

3
The Holy Spirit

Ninety times in the Old Testament, the Holy Spirit is referred to under some seventeen or eighteen different designations. Two hundred sixty times in the New Testament under some thirty designations he is mentioned. He appears immediately in the Word of God: "In the beginning God created the heaven and the earth. And the earth was without form and void; and darkness was upon the face of the deep. And the spirit of God moved upon the face of the waters" (Gen. 1:1–2). That is our introduction to the Holy Spirit. He is not defined or described; he is simply introduced. The Word of God does not explain the existence of the Holy Spirit. That is beyond our comprehension.

His Person

First of all, notice his person. We are talking about a person, not a thing. We refer to the Holy Spirit as "it" many times. Such is always erroneous. He is a person. The Bible speaks of him as a person. "Howbeit when he, the Spirit of truth, is come, he will guide you into all truth: for he shall not speak of himself; but whatsoever he shall hear, that shall he speak: and he will shew you things to come. He shall glorify me: for he shall receive of mine, and shall shew it unto you" (John 16:13–14).

We are not dealing with some vague, mysterious, neutral

spirit but with the living person of God himself. He is mentioned with other persons in such a way as to imply his own personality. "For it seemed good to the Holy Ghost, and to us, to lay upon you no greater burden than these necessary things" (Acts 15:28). In the Great Commission (Matt. 28:18–20), he is spoken of with God the Father and God the Son in such a way as to reveal that he is a person in his own right.

He has the characteristics of a person. He has a heart, for the Bible speaks of "the love of the Spirit" (Rom. 15:30). How can one love without a heart? He has a mind, for he is intelligent. He has knowledge, wisdom, and reasoning. He has a will. In his will he acts, he decides, he chooses. When Peter was resting at Joppa, the angel of God appeared to Cornelius and told him to go down to Joppa and find Simon Peter. At the same time messengers were coming from Cornelius, the Scripture says that the Spirit of God awakened Simon Peter and instructed him to prepare to meet the visitors (Acts 10:19–20). The Holy Spirit was involved in an act of the will, an act of choosing and directing.

He has all of the characteristics of a person. He teaches (Luke 12:12). He convicts of sin (John 16:8). He gives utterance (Acts 2:4). He commands (Acts 8:29). He forbids (Acts 16:6,7). He helps (Rom. 8:26). He searches (1 Cor. 2:10,11). He has all of the characteristics and actions of a person.

He is a divine person. He is called the *Holy* Spirit. Holiness is an attribute that only belongs to God. True holiness cannot belong to man. When Simon Peter confronted Ananias and Sapphira he said to the first who came, "Ananias, Satan has filled your heart. When you claimed this was the full price, you were lying to the Holy Spirit. The property was yours to sell or not, as you wished. And after selling it, it was yours to decide how much to give. How could you do a thing like this? You weren't lying to us, but to God" (Acts 5:3–4, TLB). In these two verses he is called the Holy Spirit at one moment and God the next.

Paul declared, "Know ye not that ye are the temple of God?" In other words, God dwells in us. We are his temple. "And that . . . Spirit of God dwelleth in you" (1 Cor. 3:16). He is called God and the Spirit of God at the same time in this verse. God and the Holy Spirit are interchangeable in the Word of God. He is the divine Spirit of God.

He has all the attributes of God. He is called the Spirit of life (Rom. 8:2). He is called the Spirit of truth (John 16:13). The love of the Spirit is present (Rom. 15:30). He is spoken of as having holiness (Eph. 4:30). He is everlasting (Heb. 9:14). He is omnipresent (Ps. 139:7).

He does the work of God. He does the work of creation (Gen. 1:2). He casts out demons (Matt. 12:28). He convicts of sin (John 16:8). He brings salvation to the heart (John 3:8). He is the effectual agent of the resurrection (Rom. 8:11).

His Purpose

Now look at his purpose. What does he do? I have listed six basic activities. There could be others, but these will be foundational for our understanding.

First, his activity is in revelation. Whatever is revealed of God apart from Jesus Christ is the express responsibility of the Holy Spirit. For instance, we can see God in nature.

The Bible tells us that the heavens declare the glory of God (Ps. 19:1). The Bible tells us that the earth is the Lord's and the fullness thereof (Ps. 24:1). We can see God in the world about us. The Spirit of God moved upon the confusion that reigned upon the face of the earth, and out of the confusion he brought order. In bringing order, he gave a revelation of God. God is so apparent in nature that those who

have never heard the gospel preached have enough light
to know of him (Rom. 1:19–20). If they respond to the light
they have, they will be led to additional light. That is the
Spirit of God working in revelation.

His task is to be transparent. The Holy Spirit does not
have a name. That Father has a name; the Son has a name;
why does not the Holy Spirit have a name? One may say,
"He has a name. It is Paraclete, Comforter." No, that is a
description of what he does. That is not his name. He has
no name. His task is to reveal. We have in the Godhead
God the Father, God the Son, and God the Holy Spirit. The
Holy Spirit's task is to reveal the eternal truth of God. The
Holy Spirit is transparent. He is absolutely the most significant and important factor in our relationship with God because he is the link in our lives between our hearts and
God. But he is transparent as he reveals God.

Secondly, he has the task of inspiration. The Bible is the
fruit of the Holy Spirit's work. It is the end result of what
the Holy Spirit is doing. "Knowing this first, that no prophecy
of the scripture is of any private interpretation. For the
prophecy came not in old time by the will of man: but holy
men of God spake as they were moved by the Holy Ghost"
(2 Pet. 1:20–21). The Word of God is the product of the
Spirit of God moving in godly people, inspiring them, directing them.

Some years ago I played golf with a PGA professional. I
love to play golf. I have always assumed that if I had better
golf clubs, I could play better golf. I had just bought the
most expensive set of golf clubs that Wilson makes. Those
clubs were the ones advertised as "the ones the pros play
with." I had a big red and white bag. I had everything! At
the same time, I bought my son a set of thirty-five-dollar
golf clubs. This professional golfer I was to play with did

not have his clubs with him. I insisted that he use my clubs.
He played the first nine holes with a result that was not
too good for a PGA professional!

On the second nine holes he decided to hit with my son's
clubs. He took those thirty-five-dollar clubs and shot five
under par. He was five under par for nine holes with a set
of clubs that did not cost forty dollars. It absolutely blew
my mind, but I learned something. A real pro swinging the
club is the reason the ball goes the way it goes. I can understand that. Thus it is not difficult for me to see how the
Almighty God can take human vessels and produce mighty
results. God's Word declares, "This precious treasure—this
light and power that now shine within us—is held in a perishable container, that is, in our weak bodies. Everyone can
see that the glorious power within must be from God and
is not our own" (2 Cor. 4:7, TLB). This Bible is not of any
human origin. It is the fruit, the result of the inspiration
of the Holy Spirit in the lives of these men of old. It is the
Holy Spirit who inspired the Scripture.

Thirdly, he is the agent of salvation. He is the one who
applies the redemptive work of God to our hearts. We may
wonder how the death of a man two thousand years ago
does anything for us today. The only way it does is that
the Spirit of God takes the perfect sacrifice of Jesus Christ,
lifts it out of the chronology of history, and makes it a current
reality to us today. This is a miracle of God.

In talking to Nicodemus Jesus said, "Verily, verily, I say
unto thee, Except a man be born of water and of the Spirit,
he cannot enter into the kingdom of God" (John 3:5). Then
he explained what water means. It refers to human birth
or flesh. "That which is born of the flesh is flesh. Marvel
not that I said unto thee, Ye must be born again. The wind
bloweth where it listeth, and thou hearest the sound thereof,

but canst not tell whence it cometh, and whither it goeth: so is every one that is born of the Spirit" (John 3:6,7–8). It is the Holy Spirit of God who produces salvation in our lives.

He is the one who draws us to the Father. Concerning the Holy Spirit, Jesus revealed, "It is expedient for you that I go away: for if I go not away, the Comforter will not come unto you; but if I depart, I will send him unto you. And when he is come, he will reprove the world of sin, and of righteousness, and of judgment" (John 16:7,8). His job is to convict and to draw us to the Father. He has the work of salvation.

Fourthly, he has the work of sanctification. That refers to the maturity of the believer. God does not want us to be saved and then remain spiritual babies. It is the Holy Spirit's job to make us strong, to mature us in our faith. It is the Holy Spirit who intercedes for us, who helps us in our weaknesses (Rom. 8:26). He is the one who guides us along. It is the Holy Spirit who shields us from temptation. That is the task of the Holy Spirit—sanctifying, maturing, and making holy the believer.

Fifthly, he has the task of administration. The administration of the people of God is done by the Holy Spirit. The Holy Spirit has assigned responsibilities within the church. It would be unfortunate in any business if there were not assigned responsibilities. The Holy Spirit has assigned responsibilities for the administration of the church, which is God's business. The church was born in the Spirit. We go back to Pentecost as the beginning date of the church. When Jesus left, the Holy Spirit came. Thus, the church was born by and through the Holy Spirit. That is how the church came into being. It is up to the Holy Spirit to direct the affairs of the church.

How does the Holy Spirit administer the church? The Bible reveals that he has given gifts to the church. "Now concerning spiritual gifts, brethren, I would not have you ignorant. For to one is given by the Spirit the word of wisdom; to another the word of knowledge by the same Spirit; To another faith by the same Spirit; to another the gifts of healing by the same Spirit; To another the working of miracles; to another prophecy; to another discerning of spirits; to another divers kinds of tongues; to another the interpretation of tongues: but all these worketh that one and the selfsame Spirit, dividing to every man severally as he will" (1 Cor. 12:1,8–11).

The administering of the gifts, the directing of the body of Christ is the work of the Holy Spirit. What we have to do is get back to what God has assigned us to do. There is a grand diversity of gifts administered by the Holy Spirit. If we will do it God's way, the world will be absolutely amazed at what happens through his people. God is not going to hurt us. He is not going to bring anything harmful into his church.

The pastor is assigned by the Holy Spirit to spearhead the administration of the church. "Take heed therefore unto yourselves, and to all the flock, over the which the Holy Ghost hath made you overseers, to feed the church of God" (Acts 20:28). He is to be an overseer, with the responsibility of directing the spiritual ministries of the church. When your church called your pastor, you just agreed with God on it. God assigned him to you, and you agreed with God on the assignment. The task of our churches is to agree with the Holy Spirit. "As they ministered to the Lord, and fasted, the Holy Ghost said, Separate me Barnabas and Saul for the work whereunto I have called them. And when they had fasted and prayed, and laid their hands on them, they sent them away" (Acts 13:2–3).

The Holy Spirit's assigning, directing, and administering was the key to the effectiveness of the early church. God has a great manifestation of his power and his glory that he will demonstrate to people who will agree with him in the administration of the Holy Spirit.

There is a sixth thing that the Holy Spirit is here to do. He has the work of representation. He is a representative. He does not represent himself. He is not his own agent. He is here to represent Jesus (John 16:13–14). When Jesus is real to us, the Holy Spirit is doing his work. Everything the Bible tells us about Jesus was given to us by the Holy Spirit. Jesus is precious and real to us because the Holy Spirit is doing his job. Paul said emphatically that "no man can say that Jesus is the Lord, but by the Holy Ghost" (1 Cor. 12:3). He is never more active in us than when he is revealing Jesus Christ to us. When we rejoice in the presence of Jesus Christ, it is the Holy Spirit drawing us to him.

4
Jesus Christ

Jesus Christ is the perfect revelation of God. He is the express image and exact essence of God. He is the central figure in the Word of God. Remove Jesus Christ from God's redemptive purposes, and there is nothing left but an empty shell. What we believe about Jesus Christ is significant. If we acknowledge the truth that Jesus Christ is the divine, eternal Son of God, we have placed ourselves where God can move into our lives. If we identify Jesus as simply a good teacher, a moral man, one of many sons of God, we eliminate any possibility that we will ever enter into forgiveness of sins and salvation. What we believe about Jesus Christ is absolutely pivotal in our relationship with God.

God declared concerning Jesus, "This is my beloved Son, in whom I am well pleased" (Matt. 3:17). The beloved apostle John gave a beautiful presentation of the person of Jesus Christ:

"Before anything else existed, there was Christ, with God. He has always been alive and is himself God. He created everything there is—nothing exists that he didn't make. Eternal life is in him, and this life gives light to all mankind. His life is the light that shines through the darkness—and the darkness can never extinguish it. God sent John the Baptist as a witness to the fact that Jesus Christ is the true Light. John himself was not the Light; he was only a witness to identify it. Later on, the one who is the true Light arrived

38

to shine on everyone coming into the world. But although he made the world, the world didn't recognize him when he came. Even in his own land and among his own people, the Jews, he was not accepted. Only a few would welcome and receive him. But to all who received him, he gave the right to become children of God. All they needed to do was to trust him to save them. All those who believe this are reborn!—not a physical rebirth resulting from human passion or plan—but from the will of God" (John 1:1–13, TLB).

It is interesting that Luke, a physician, was the one who told us about the virgin birth. "Dear Friend who loves God: Several biographies of Christ have already been written using as their source material the reports circulating among us from the early disciples and other eyewitnesses. However, it occurred to me that it would be well to recheck all these accounts from first to last and after thorough investigation to pass this summary on to you, to reassure you of the truth of all you were taught" (Luke 1:1–4, TLB). Luke declared that God had given him a clear picture of the facts as they really were.

No more comprehensive view of the birth and early life of Jesus do we have than in Luke's Gospel. He revealed that God gave him perfect understanding and insight to write these things "to reassure you of the truth of all you were taught" (Luke 1:4, TLB).

Almost everything we know about Jesus Christ we learn from the Word of God. Any experience with Jesus that is inconsistent with the Bible needs to be reexamined.

The Eternal Son

He is the eternal Son of God. Jesus said, "The absolute truth is that I was in existence before Abraham was ever born" (John 8:58, TLB). As Jesus was praying he said, "And now, Father, reveal my glory as I stand in your presence, the glory we shared before the world began" (John 17:5, TLB). Jesus lived before he was born. He is the eternal Son of God. He is called a coequal with God. "In the beginning was the Word, and the Word was with God, and the Word was God" (John 1:1). In the original language the word *the* is not there. The Scripture literally says, "in beginning."

We can think of any beginning we desire; and whenever we can think of a beginning, Jesus was already there. He existed before any beginning. He preexisted the bringing of order out of chaos in Genesis. He preexisted the creation of man. He is the eternal Son of God.

Jesus is divine. Jesus declared, "I and my Father are one" (John 10:30). In Hebrews 1:1–3 he is called the same essence as God. Throughout the New Testament, God and Christ are linked on equal terms. Many times God and Jesus Christ are linked as plural subjects with a singular verb. This means they act as one. They are one and the same essence. Jesus Christ, the eternal Son of God, is divine!

The Bible also points out the other side of that truth. Jesus Christ was also human. He was born as a baby and, like other babies, had normal human needs. He had to be cared for. He had to have someone feed him and nurture him. He needed someone to teach him. He had a family. He grew to maturity in a particular area. Everything about being human that would be true of us was true of Jesus. He spoke of himself as being man. Other people spoke of him as a man.

In the message that Simon Peter preached at Pentecost he said, "Ye men of Israel, hear these words; Jesus of Nazareth, a man approved of God among you by miracles and wonders and signs" (Acts 2:22). The apostle Paul declared, "For if through the offence of one many be dead, much more the grace of God, and the gift by grace which is by one man, Jesus Christ, hath abounded unto many" (Rom. 5:15). Jesus said, "But now ye seek to kill me, a man who told you the truth, which I have heard of God" (John 8:40).

It is important for us to understand the humanity of Jesus Christ. He prayed as a man. He was tempted as a man. The book of Hebrews talks at length about the fact that he was tempted in all manners as we are tempted. Thus he suffered all the things we suffer. He is our high priest who can be touched with our infirmity (Heb. 4:15). Hebrews 2:14 says, "Forasmuch then as the children are partakers of flesh and blood, he also himself likewise took part of the same."

Jesus Christ was human! He was divine! The uniqueness of Jesus was that he blended in one person perfect manhood and perfect deity. He was everything man could want God to be and everything God could want man to be. Perfect God—perfect man. He was human just as we are, yet divine.

The Bible further reveals that he was born of a virgin. "These are the facts concerning the birth of Jesus Christ: His mother, Mary was engaged to be married to Joseph. But while she was still a virgin she became pregnant by the Holy Spirit. Then Joseph, her fiancé, being a man of stern principle, decided to break the engagement but to do it quietly, as he didn't want to publicly disgrace her" (Matt. 1:18–19, TLB). Jewish law declared that if an engaged woman became pregnant, she could be stoned to death or disposed of privately. Joseph loved Mary greatly and wanted to do what was right. So, when he found out she was to have a child, it was in his heart to put her away privately so there would be a minimum of embarrassment and public shame.

"But while he thought on these things, behold, the angel

of the Lord appeared unto him in a dream, saying, Joseph, thou son of David, fear not to take unto thee Mary thy wife: for that which is conceived in her is of the Holy Ghost. And she shall bring forth a son and thou shalt call his name JESUS: for he shall save his people from their sins. Now all this was done, that it might be fulfilled which was spoken of the Lord by prophet, saying, Behold, a virgin shall be with child, and shall bring forth a son, and they shall call his name Emmanuel, which being interpreted is, God with us. Then Joseph being raised from sleep did as the angel of the Lord had bidden him, and took unto him his wife: And knew her not till she had brought forth her firstborn son: and he called his name JESUS" (Matt. 1:20–25).

Some have said that in ancient pagan literature and mythology there were stories of special births in which a woman on earth would give birth to the child of a god. The pagan stories were abundant and very evident. But the story of the virgin birth of Jesus did not come out of pagan folklore. It came out of a conservative Jewish community that did not accept pagan folklore. The pagan legends were stories of gods who came to earth and cohabited with the women on earth. These births were not virgin at all. They were simply the products of divine and human sexual encounters. But the Gospels state that in this case there was no sexual relationship of any kind, natural or supernatural. God simply planted a seed in Mary, and Jesus was conceived. There was no sexual passion involved. The Holy Spirit planted the seed of Jesus Christ in the womb of virgin Mary. That seed united with her seed, and Jesus was born from a girl in her teens who had never known any sexual relation whatsoever. That is a miracle of God. That is why he is both divine and human.

It is Jesus' virgin birth that makes it possible for Jesus to be the Christ and the Messiah. Take away the virgin birth and we have eliminated the place of Jesus Christ in the plan of redemption. The virgin birth affirmed his humanity. He was born of a woman. It affirms his deity, for he was conceived of the Holy Spirit (Luke 1:35).

Paul said, "God was in Christ, reconciling the world unto himself" (2 Cor. 5:19). And John announced, "The word was made flesh and dwelt among us" (John 1:14). We are not discussing fairy tales! In the midst of all the delusions, the illusions, and the confusion, God has come. God has invaded human history. God has come in the form of a man. That is the incarnation. Jesus Christ, perfectly God, perfectly man, has entered the arena of human history.

The Sinless Son

He is also the sinless son of God. John said, "Ye know that he was manifested to take away our sins; and in him is no sin" (1 John 3:5). From the cross one of the thieves said, "And we indeed [suffered] justly; for we receive the due reward of our deeds: but this man hath done nothing amiss" (Luke 23:41). We cannot find an error in the life of Jesus. He never said a word that should have been erased. He never took a step that he would want to retrace. He never did anything amiss.

We do not find anywhere in the Gospels where he prayed for forgiveness or confessed a sin. Indeed, he challenged his enemies to find any fault in him.

Sinlessness is not just negative. That does not mean just the absence of sin. It means positive excellence of character. One of the real tragedies in our lives occurs when we measure our goodness by what we do not do! Certainly sinlessness involves what we do not do; but it also involves what we do. The pattern of Jesus' life was one of obedience. He obeyed God. That is firm evidence that he was sinless. Our greatest sins are not the acts that we commit in rebellion against God by our personal practice. Our greatest sins are the things we refuse to do because we have rebelled against God. "To him that knoweth to do good, and doeth it not, to him it is sin" (James 4:17).

Jesus was one who had no sin in him, either negatively or positively. He did not simply fail to commit sin, but there were positive elements and characteristics of sinlessness in his life. He was excellent in character. He was what God wanted him to be so that God could say, "I am pleased with him."

The Suffering Son

He is the suffering Son of God. "For Christ also hath once suffered for sins, the just for the unjust, that he might bring us to God, being put to death in the flesh, but quickened by the Spirit" (1 Pet. 3:18). The beautiful passage in Isaiah that deals with his death upon the cross and its meaning for our redemption declares, "Surely he hath borne our griefs, and carried our sorrows: yet we did esteem him stricken, smitten of God, and afflicted. But he was wounded for our transgressions, he was bruised for our iniquities: the chastisement of our peace was upon him; and with his stripes we are healed. All we like sheep have gone astray; we have turned every one to his own way; and the Lord hath laid on him the iniquity of us all. He was oppressed, and he was afflicted . . ." (Isa. 43:4-7).

The writer of Hebrews revealed that God ordained "to make the captain of . . . salvation perfect through sufferings" (Heb. 2:10). We cannot understand the person of Jesus Christ unless we understand that he is the suffering Son of God. That means his death upon the cross—a death he did not deserve. He was sinless. Thus he could be the perfect sacrifice for sin.

Let us examine his death for a moment. First of all, it was substitutionary. It was for us! When speaking about the Lord's Supper, Jesus said, "This is my blood of the new testament, which is shed for many for the remission of sins" (Matt. 26:28). Ponder Jesus' death upon the cross. Watch the agony build in his soul. Observe that agony as it expresses itself in his prayer in the garden: "Abba, Father, all things are possible unto thee: take away this cup from me" (Mark 14:36). He struggled and wrestled with the agony of a world's sin.

Now watch him hanging there on the cross and see the pressure as it builds in his soul until it explodes from within and he cries, "My God, my God, why hast thou forsaken me?" (Mark 15:34). And when we see that, just know that his suffering was for us. That cry was in our behalf! When he cried out from the depths of the pressure of sin upon his soul, it was for you and for me.

His death was voluntary. It was by his own choice. Jesus said of his life, "No man taketh it from me, but I lay it down of myself. I have power to lay it down, and I have power to take it again. This commandment have I received of my Father" (John 10:18). He gave his life for us of his own choice.

Further, his death is sufficient for all of us. We do not need Jesus Christ *and* baptism *and/or* church membership. We do not need Jesus Christ *and* "do the best you can." We do not need Jesus Christ and/or anything. We need Jesus Christ, period! The beloved apostle John said, "He is the propitiation for our sins: and not for ours only, but also for the sins of the whole world" (1 John 2:2). When one person is saved, it does not diminish the ability of Jesus to save somebody else! His death is sufficient. Hebrews declares, "He is able also to save them to the uttermost who come unto God by him" (Heb. 7:25). He has sufficient power to atone for every one of our sins.

The Victorious Son

Jesus is also the victorious son of God. The apostle Paul declared, "Wherefore God also hath highly exalted him, and given him a name which is above every name: That at the name of Jesus every knee should bow, of things in heaven, and things in earth, and things under the earth; And that every tongue should confess that Jesus Christ is Lord, to the glory of God the Father" (Phil. 2:9–11). He is the victorious son of God.

He is the interceding son of God. After we read that he is able to save to the uttermost, we read, "He ever liveth to make intercession for them" (Heb. 7:25). He is praying for us. He is interceding in our behalf. He is our advocate. The victorious King is our lawyer. He is our intercessor.

The Bible tells us this victorious son is not only risen and interceding, but he is returning. The victorious Son is also reigning and ruling. He is King! "I saw heaven opened, and behold a white horse; and he that sat upon him was called Faithful and True, and in righteousness he doth judge and make war. His eyes were as a flame of fire, and on this head were many crowns; and he had a name written, that no man knew, but he himself. And he was clothed with a vesture dipped in blood: and his name is called The Word of God. And the armies which were in heaven followed him upon white horses, clothed in fine linen, white and clean. And out of his mouth goeth a sharp sword, that with it he should smite the nations: and he shall rule them with a rod of iron: and he treadeth the winepress of the fierceness and wrath of Almighty God. And he hath on his vesture and on his thigh a name written, KING OF KINGS, AND LORD OF LORDS" (Rev. 19:11–16). This Jesus is the reigning king. He is the eternal Son of God—divine, human, virgin born, sinless, suffering, and victorious.

The most exciting truth about Jesus is not that he is a historical personality. The Bible tells us that the historical Jesus who is one day returning to establish his kingdom can come and live in our hearts right now. That is what Christianity is. Christianity is Jesus Christ. Christianity is walking in the power of his Spirit and his presence. We can know him for ourselves. We can know that he dwells within us. As he does, he will live his life through us day by day. The eternal Son of God can come and be at home in our hearts today.

5
The Trinity

Wherever a church or group of churches have abandoned or obscured the doctrine of the trinity, they have very quickly lost every other characteristic doctrine of the gospel. Heresy of all kinds has come in. The doctrine of the trinity is vital in our understanding of God, of salvation, and of redemption.

The Scriptural Claim

First, what is the scriptural claim? The list of verses that refer to the three-in-one nature of God is lengthy. Concerning the redemption of mankind through Jesus Christ, the apostle Paul said, "All things are of God, who hath reconciled us to himself by Jesus Christ, and hath given to us the ministry of reconciliation; To wit, that God was in Christ, reconciling the world unto himself" (2 Cor. 5:18–19). At one moment he said that God was reconciling us unto himself *by* Jesus Christ, and in the next moment said that he was *in* Jesus Christ so reconciling. When Jesus declares that those who are saved are held safely in his hand and that those given to him by the Father are not able to be plucked out of the Father's hand, he says, "I and my Father are one" (John 10:30).

In Romans Paul said, "Ye are not in the flesh, but in the Spirit, if so be that the Spirit of God dwell in you. Now if

48

any man have not the Spirit of Christ . . ." (Rom. 8:9). In
the same verse he is called the Spirit of God and the Spirit
of Christ. Which is he? Is he Spirit of God or Spirit of Christ?
Indeed, he is both. In verse 10: "Christ be in you . . ."
How can Christ be in us? Through his Spirit! In verse 11:
"If the Spirit of him that raised up Jesus . . . ." Now the
Spirit of God raised up Jesus. We have all three persons in
focus again. In verse 14: "As many as are led by the Spirit
of God." In verse 15: "Ye have received the Spirit of adoption." And in verse 16: "The Spirit itself beareth witness
with our spirit." In Colossians 1:15,19 Paul said, "Who is
the image of the invisible God, the firstborn of every creature. For it pleased the Father that in him should all fulness
dwell." If all fullness dwells in Jesus, then all of God is in
Jesus and Jesus is all of God. "In the beginning was the
Word, and the Word was with God, and the Word was God"
(John 1:1).

The scriptural claim is that God is three in one, one in
three: God the Father, God the Holy Spirit, and God the
Son. The Bible ascribes divine titles to Christ. He is called
God. The perfections that belong only to God are ascribed
to Jesus. The Bible ascribes divine works to Christ. And beyond this, the Bible admonishes man to give supreme worship to Jesus.

The Bible ascribes divine attributes to the Holy Spirit.
The Holy Spirit is described in the same characteristics, the
same attributes as God himself. Divine works and divine
purposes are ascribed to the Holy Spirit. Divine character
is also ascribed to the Holy Spirit. Clearly the Scripture
claims that there are three, yet one—one, yet three. Each
member of the Godhead has meaning only in relation to
the other members of the Godhead. Each one must be God
because each one is dependent upon the other for his full

expression. We cannot understand God without understanding him as God the Father, God the Son, God the Holy Spirit. The three attributes, the three essences, the three expressions are necessary for us to have God in all of his fullness and completeness. And yet there is unity there. They are not conflicting concepts. They are complementary. They are not exclusive of each other. They are inclusive of each other.

Basically, the doctrine of the trinity is the result of the recognition of the deity of Christ. If Jesus is the divine, then there must be two essences in the Godhead. For one to be God, he has to be supreme. If Jesus is God and God is God, then there are either two Gods or we have two expressions of one God. Out of the recognition that Jesus was not only the Son of God but was indeed God himself has grown the understanding of the trinity. Father, Son, and Holy Spirit all have prominent places in the Bible.

"The Word [Jesus] was with God, and the Word was God. The same was in the beginning with God. All things were made by him; and without him was not any thing made that was made" (John 1:1–3). "In the beginning God created the heaven and the earth. And the earth was without form and void . . . And the spirit of God moved upon the face of the waters" (Gen. 1:1,2). And in the book of Hebrews, there is that tremendous description of Christ. "God . . . hath . . . spoken unto us by his Son, whom he hath appointed heir of all things, by whom also he made the worlds; Who being the brightness of his glory, and the express image of his person" (Heb. 1:1–3). Jesus is ascribed the same character and essence of God himself.

The Bible speaks of three in one, one in three. There are not three Gods, but only one God. Yet there are three distinct expressions by which we know God.

The Rational Examples

Let us look at some rational examples. There are some things that can help us understand this three-in-one nature of God. They cannot prove the concept to us, but they can help us to understand.

First is the example of man himself. We are composed of three parts. We are body; we are soul; and we are spirit. The body is our physical contact with the real world. It is the world as felt by our senses. We are a body. We are also a spirit. The spirit is not material-conscious; it is self-conscious. We know ourselves by our spirit, by our personalities. In our spirit we have God-consciousness. We do not have God-consciousness in the soul or in the body. We have some hints, but God-consciousness comes in the spirit. In the spirit we respond to God. In the spirit we adore God and worship God.

Now, we are three! Yet we are not ourselves without all three. If the body dies, we are not ourselves as we understand ourselves. We are diverse persons, yet we are united persons. The tremendous rise in psychiatrists and psychologists and mental institutions has occurred because of the fragmenting of the unity of personhood. We were not meant to be fragmented. Holiness literally means wholeness, the whole personality moving together in the same direction.

We are body, soul, and spirit. We are each one of those things, and we are all of them combined. We are one; we are three. God is the perfection of what we see in ourselves. God is the perfection of the physical—Jesus Christ. God is the perfection of the soul—the Holy Spirit. He is the perfection of that which we find in ourselves. Man is three distinct essences, yet one person. The same thing is true of God, only multipled to infinity and made perfect.

A very simple and elementary example would be the example of water. Water is made up of two parts hydrogen and one part oxygen. If we freeze it, it is a solid. If we leave it at normal temperature it is a liquid; and if we boil it, it becomes a vapor. Yet no matter whether it is ice, liquid, or vapor, it is still two parts hydrogen, one part oxygen. It has three distinct characteristics, three distinct expressions; yet it is one and the same essence.

The Practical Expressions

Note now the practical expressions. These are statements derived from the Word of God relative to God the Father, God the Holy Spirit, and God the Son.

The work of Christ and the work of the Holy Spirit is just as much the work of God as the work of the Father. Wherever Christ works, God is working. Wherever the Holy Spirit works, God is working. In Christ we find God. Yet the revelation of God is made real to us only by the work of the Holy Spirit. The Bible makes it clear that in knowing Christ, we know God. God is in Christ, reconciling the world unto himself. To know God, we must know Christ. That is not possible except by the Holy Spirit. We can see why we need Father, Son, and Holy Spirit.

Paul declared, "If you will confess that Jesus is Lord and believe that God raised him from death, you will be saved" (Rom. 10:9, TEV). Elsewhere Paul said, "No man can say that Jesus is the Lord but by the Holy Ghost" (1 Cor. 12:3). We need the Holy Spirit to reveal Christ and to show us God. We need them together. In Romans 8 we read that the Holy Spirit bears witness with our spirit that we are the children of God. The Holy Spirit reveals to us that we are saved. We could never know that we are children of God and heirs of God apart from the Holy Spirit.

By faith in Christ, through the power of the Holy Spirit,

we know God as our Father. We cannot identify God absolutely as Father, Son, or Holy Spirit. It takes each of these to complete the concept of God. The Father is the source and the origin of all things. The Son is the medium of the outgoing energy and power of God. The Holy Spirit works to complete all things.

There is another very practical understanding. The Bible claims that God is love. If God is love, when did he become love? Does that mean that God has always been love? If God has always been love, how can we have love without an object of love? So, if God has always been love, and love is eternal, then there must have been an object of his love before he ever created the universe. There must be, within the Godhead, an object of God's love for God to eternally be love as the Scripture claims that he is. He did not become love when he created man. An adequate object of love must be found in the Godhead and not in the created universe. The Bible tells us that Jesus the Son was the object of God's love long before this physical universe was ever created.

The Position of Faith

Consider now the position of faith. One may ask, "Can you prove to me this matter of the trinity?" No, I cannot. Ultimately, the concept of God as three in one, one in three has to be received by faith. By faith, I accept the doctrine of the trinity. The true God has revealed himself to us through the Scripture. The only God we can know is the God who has revealed himself through the Scripture. If we are to know him correctly, we must know him precisely as he has revealed himself in the Scripture. If we do not accept what he has revealed about himself in the Scripture, then we will be left with a false and heretical concept of God.

The entire plan of redemption in all of its parts is founded upon this doctrine of the trinity. Justification—the work of God in bringing redemption—is made possible only by the shed blood of Jesus Christ upon the cross. Without the Son, there can be no justification. Sanctification is made possible by the application of the shed blood of Christ and the eternal truth of his Word through the Holy Spirit in our lives. We cannot grow and mature and be sanctified without the Holy Spirit. Adoption—the relationship that places me in a Father-son relationship with God—would not be possible without the Father. Everything basic to Christian truth centers and hinges on my trust and my confidence that God is Father, Son, and Holy Spirit.

Some may ask, "What difference does it make?" First, it makes a geat deal of difference as far as the integrity of God is concerned. God has said it, and we believe in his integrity. Secondly, an understanding of this will make it possible for us to comprehend a relationship with God. We need a God we can see. He is Jesus, the Son. There needs to be a sacrifice made for sin. That sacrifice was the sinless Son of God. There must be a continuing fellowship with God the Father. That is made possible through his Holy Spirit.

There must be a divine purpose, will, and direction for our lives. That is made possible because of the intelligence and creative genius of God the Father. God the Father projects, through Jesus Christ's sacrifice and through the Holy Spirit, his will and purposes in me. Thus, we know God not as three gods but as one, yet in three expressions. God is the Father; God is the Son; and God is the Holy Spirit. God set up that plan so that he might relate to us and reveal himself to us.

6
The Nature of Man

Man is a complex person. He exists. Yet how does he exist?
What is he? He can tell his hand to do something and his
hand responds, but his hand is not the one who decides
what to do. His hand is not himself. He has a brain. His
brain is his, but not him. When we speak of existing, we
are saying that we have an ability to know, to have understanding that is separate from everything physical about us.
I may lose my arm, but I still exist as perfectly as if I had
the arm. When we look at our being, there is something
there that defies logic. When we have taken away everything
we can see about us, we still exist. Man is a complex study.
Volumes have been written about it. For our purpose, we
will simply look at what the Bible says about man, what
we are like, who we are, what lies ahead, and what our
purpose is.

"And God said, Let us make man in our image, after our
likeness: and let them have dominion over the fish of the
sea, and over the fowl of the air, and over the cattle, and
over all the earth, over every creeping thing that creepeth
upon the earth. So God created man in his own image, in
the image of God created he him; male and female created
he them. And God blessed them, and God said unto them,
Be fruitful, and multiply, and replenish the earth, and subdue it: and have dominion over the fish of the sea, and over

the fowl of the air, and over every living thing that moveth upon the earth" (Gen. 1:26–28).

With that simple explanation, mankind appears upon the earth.

The Creation of Man

We will not try to defend or to explain the doctrine of creation. We will simply accept the Bible teaching that man is the result of the deliberate creation of God. Man is no freak of nature. He is no accident upon the universal scene. He is the deliberate result of the intelligence, wisdom, and love of God. "The Lord God caused the man to fall into a deep sleep, and took one of his ribs and closed up the place from which he had removed it, and made the rib into a woman, and brought her to the man. 'This is it!' Adam exclaimed. 'She is part of my own bone and flesh! Her name is "woman" because she was taken out of a man'" (Gen. 2:21–23, TLB). All of this creation is by design. God initiated the appearance of man upon the earth.

"I cannot understand how you can bother with mere puny man, to pay any attention to him! And yet you have made him only a little lower than the angels, and placed a crown of glory and honor upon his head" (Ps. 8:4–5, TLB). That is still an amazement. Think about the fact that there are four billion people on the earth. A billion is more than our minds can comprehend. There have not been one billion minutes since Jesus died. Yet there are four billion people on the earth today. It would be easy for us in a computerized age to say, "What value is man that God would even consider him?"

The reason is this: "Thou madest him a little lower than the angels; thou crownedst him with glory and honour, and didst set him over the works of thy hands: Thou hast put all things in subjection under his feet" (Heb. 2:7–8). With deliberate forethought, with explicit design, and with ultimate wisdom, God created man. Without man, creation has no meaning whatsoever.

The Genesis account tells us that man was the climax of creation. He was the highest order of creation. If we were to remove man from the earth, we would have a nonsensical existence. All of creation finds its meaning, its sense, its purpose as it relates to man.

Man was made in the image of God (Gen. 1:27). That phrase is tossed about and discussed freely, but what does it mean? When man was made, he had immediate fellowship with God. There was something of God in man because immediately God and man were friends. There was immediate communion and fellowship.

This means that man has intelligence. Man has the ability to be a rational, thinking person. Man has the ability to assimilate knowledge and understand truth. This ability gives man the capacity to develop astounding intellectual understanding. That in itself is part of being made in the image of God.

More than that, we have free will. Nobody forces us to do anything. They can influence us. They may make it appealing and attractive. They may make it difficult for us to say no or yes, but no one can force man. Man uniquely has free will. His body may be mastered, and he may be in chains as an animal; but he has a will that cannot be conquered apart from himself. He has free will, free choice. Nothing else in creation has that capacity.

He can choose to love. He has the unique ability to be rational in his affections. The animal kingdom has instinctive affection. There is an affection that the animals have. A dog may love his master. He may do what his master tells him to do. His master may teach him to respond to certain commands. But only man can look up to God and say, "O Lord, my God, how great thou art. I love you." Animals cannot do that. The ability to love God and man by rational choice is part of the image of God in man.

Man has a moral sense about him. The animal kingdom does not have any morality. God placed a sense of moral values in man. The rest of creation only knows amorality. We know morality and immorality. The morality of man is part of being made in the image of God.

Another aspect of being made in the image of God is that God made man to have dominion. Man was told to subdue the earth and to have dominion over it. God gave us the world. God instructed us to conquer it and have dominion over it. Every time we achieve something that astonishes our minds, that is just more of the fulfillment of the command God gave uniquely to man: to have dominion, to conquer, to subdue the earth.

In pursuing this matter of man's creation, we need to examine the trichotomy of creation. Man is body, spirit, and soul.

Man is a body. Body refers to that part of man which is controlled by the five senses—what we can see, hear, taste, smell, and touch. This is our world consciousness. Every one of us has been created by God to be conscious of the world about us.

Man is a body, and he is a soul. The soul is the seat of our emotions. It is in our souls that we have our appetites and our affections. It is in our souls that we have our personalities. The soul is what we are. Man has a body, but man is a soul. The soul is our self-consciousness. I am conscious of me. I am the center of my world. I cannot imagine a world without me. You cannot imagine a world without you. We are conscious of ourselves. Every other consciousness proceeds from that.

Man is not only body and soul, but he is also spirit. Spirit is the deepest, most eternal part of the makeup of mankind. It is in the spirit that we love God. It is in the spirit that we worship God. It is the spirit that has God-consciousness. God created us to have a body so that we would be conscious of the world about us. He created us to have a soul so that we would be conscious of ourselves and have unique personalities. He created us to have a spirit so that we would be conscious of him.

The Degeneration of Man

The Bible speaks of man's degeneration. When Adam and Eve sinned, they fell from the perfect state of fellowship with God. Before they sinned, they had perfect fellowship with God. They walked with God. They talked with God. But that fellowship was broken. Man became degenerate.

Man turned away from God and became totally depraved. Total depravity does not mean that man is as bad as he can get. Total depravity means that every part of man's being fell when Adam fell. When Adam sinned, his whole being was corrupted. A schism in his personality resulted. His body, his spirit, and his soul were torn apart, and he fragmented himself. Total depravity means that every part is tainted by sin.

"Let me say this, then, speaking for the Lord: Live no longer as the unsaved do, for they are blinded and confused. Their closed hearts are full of darkness; they are far away from the life of God because they have shut their minds against him, and they cannot understand his ways" (Eph.

4:17–18, TLB). The soul is debased; the spirit is darkened. All man's being is affected. The body is diseased and subject to death and decay.

Paul spoke of his body as being the "body of . . . death" (Rom. 7:24). Total depravity means that my body is affected by the fall. Total depravity means that the conscience is blunted. The apostle Paul spoke about those "having their conscience seared with a hot iron" (1 Tim. 4:2). The conscience of man is not reliable because it has been seared and blunted. Just because we do not feel guilty about some things does not mean that they are right. We can train our consciences to accept what we do without guilt.

Total depravity means that, spiritually, we are dead (Eph. 2:1). We are under judgment from God. "The Lord Jesus shall be revealed from heaven with his mighty angels, In flaming fire taking vengeance on them that know not God, and that obey not the gospel of our Lord Jesus Christ: Who shall be punished with ever lasting destruction from the presence of the Lord, and from the glory of his power" (2 Thess. 1:7–9). Man is under judgment and guilty before God; for all have sinned. None of us is righteous. Our hearts are deceitful and desperately wicked. When we speak of being totally depraved, we mean that every facet of our lives has fallen and has been corrupted by sin.

Look now at the results of the fall. When man fell, sin became universal. "When Adam sinned, sin entered the entire human race. His sin spread death throughout all the world, so everything began to grow old and die, for all sinned" (Rom. 5:12, TLB). We inherit Adam's guilt. We inherit his tendency to sin. There is a great deal of difference between original sin and actual sin. We are guilty under God because of original sin. We have a sinful nature that will rebel against God. That is not to say that children are held accountable because God has provided for them until they reach an age of understanding. The Bible says that every child, regardless of how well he may be trained, when he reaches an age of understanding, will choose to sin and thus will need to be saved. We are guilty by original sin and actual sin and thus need to be forgiven. Sin became universal as a result of man's fall.

Secondly, death became universal. God never intended for us to die. God never intended for the body to decay and die. That was the penalty of sin. Through the fall death became universal.

Further, when man fell, he lost fellowship with God. "Listen now! The Lord isn't too weak to save you. And he isn't getting deaf! He can hear you when you call! But the trouble is that your sins have cut you off from God. Because of sin he has turned his face away from you and will not listen anymore" (Isa. 59:1–2, TLB). Sin has made it impossible for us to have fellowship with God. As soon as Adam and Eve sinned, fellowship was broken. God did not do anything; they did. They knew something had happened. They hid themselves. God, who had been a delight and a joy to them, was now to be feared.

Man was now under the condemnation of God. "For as many as are of the works of the law are under the curse: for it is written, Cursed is every one that continueth not in all things which are written in the book of the law to do them" (Gal. 3:10). Every man stands under the judgment and the condemnation of God. One of the results of the fall was the tremendous sorrow that we experience in our world. Why is there sorrow and heartbreak? It is because of man's deliberate rebellion against God. "The joy of our hearts has ended; our dance has turned to death. Our glory is gone. The crown is fallen from our head. Woe upon us

for our sins. Our hearts are faint and weary; our eyes grow
dim" (Lam. 5:15–17, TLB). The sadness and the sorrow that
we experience in this earth is because of the sinfulness of
mankind.

The ultimate result of the fall is eternal punishment. "Then
will I turn to those on my left and say, "Away with you,
you cursed ones, into the eternal fire prepared for the devil
and his demons" (Matt. 25:41, TLB). The fall created an
enmity between man and God. Unless Jesus Christ is allowed
to forgive the sin and to restore the lost image of God in
man, man will be eternally separated from God.

The Restoration of Man

The Bible also speaks of man's restoration. I am glad the
fall is not the end. It is the darkest, saddest, most bitter
story we could possibly read. But the Bible does not stop
there. The Bible not only speaks of the creation of man
and the degeneration of man, but it also speaks of the restoration of man.

God can repair the broken image. God can restore that
which has been tainted by sin. "For whom he did foreknow,
he also did predestinate to be conformed to the image of
his Son, that he might be the firstborn among many brethren" (Rom. 8:29). That image that was lost in the fall can
be restored through Jesus Christ. "Know ye not that the
unrighteous shall not inherit the kingdom of God? Be not
deceived: neither fornicators, nor idolators, nor adulterers,
nor effeminate, nor abusers of themselves with mankind,
Nor thieves, nor covetous, nor drunkards, nor revilers, nor
extortioners, shall inherit the kingdom of God. And such
were some of you: but ye are washed, but ye are sanctified,
but ye are justified in the name of the Lord Jesus, and by
the spirit of our God" (1 Cor. 6:9–11). That is good news!

We were once listed in that line of sinners. There is not any evil deed that we will not commit. We are evil by nature, by choice, and by conduct. We are not what we ought to be. "None of these will inherit the kingdom of God . . . but ye are washed, ye are sanctified, but ye are justified." God is able to take our rebellion and make sweet fellowship out of it. He is able to restore the lost image in man.

Man is not as he was created. God created two people, and he was perfectly delighted with them until they sinned. He did not make us the way we are; our sins did. But he will remake us the way we ought to be if we will let him. "That which is born of the flesh is flesh; and that which is born of the Spirit is spirit. Marvel not that I said unto thee, Ye must be born again" (John 3:6–7). That phrase "must be born again" literally means to be born anew or to be born from above. That is something man cannot do. It is something only God can do. God can take man, fallen and depraved, and he can pull the life together. He can bring forgiveness, harmony, wholeness, and completeness. God can restore that which has been robbed from us in the fall. "If any man be in Christ, he is a new creature: old things are passed away; behold all things are become new" (2 Cor. 5:17). God can recreate us and make us what we ought to be.

7
God's Infallible Word

This doctrine is basic to everything that we believe. If one denies the infallibility of the Word of God, every other doctrine in which we believe is destroyed. If the Bible is rejected, no system of belief based upon the Bible can be valid. Our faith begins with a basic commitment to and acceptance of the Bible as the infallible Word of God.

The word *Bible* comes through the French language to us by way of Latin and Greek. It originally was a word used to describe the container of precious writings. Eventually it came to refer to the sacred writings of those who call themselves Christians. We divide it into the Old Testament and the New Testament. The word *testament* simply means covenant or contract. The Old Testament is the old covenant between God and man. The New Testament is the new covenant.

The earliest Bible did not have chapters and verses. It may surprise some to realize that the chapter divisions and verse divisions are not inspired as the rest of the Bible is. There are times when a chapter ends and there is a very clear continuation of thought in the first verses of the next chapter. The divisions are not always consistent with the thought of the passage.

In the year 1227, Stephen Langton, who was professor at the University of Paris and later was the Archbishop of

Canterbury, divided the Bible into chapters. Until then, it was like a great scroll with endless numbers of lines and paragraphs. This made it very difficult to find specific passages. Finally in 1555 the verses were put in by a man named Robert Stephenus, who was a printer in the city of Paris.

Christian and Jewish scholars alike have accepted joyfully the chapter and verse divisions because of the ease that it allows us to have in approaching the study of the Word of God.

The Revealed Word

The Bible is the revealed word of God. That simply means that it is the product of divine revelation. If God does not reveal himself to us, we can never know him. We have no capacity to find him. We may search for God, but we will never find him except as he reveals himself to us. The Bible is his self-disclosure. Through it God has revealed his own being. The Bible is the divine revelation of God to us. "This salvation was something the prophets did not fully understand. Though they wrote about it, they had many questions as to what it all could mean. They wondered what the Spirit of Christ within them was talking about, for he told them to write down the events which, since then, have happened to Christ: his suffering, and his great glory afterwards. And they wondered when and to whom all this would happen" (1 Pet. 1:10–11, TLB).

God revealed to men of olden times what was going to happen through Jesus Christ. They could not have known it except through the revelation of God. The apostle Peter continued, "They were finally told that these things would not occur during their lifetime, but long years later, during yours. And now at last this Good News has been plainly announced to all of us. It was preached to us in the power of the same heaven-sent Holy Spirit who spoke to them; and it is all so strange and wonderful that even the angels in heaven would give a great deal to know more about it" (1 Pet. 1:12, TLB).

The Inspired Word

When we talk about the inspiration of the Scriptures, we are not talking about someone like Milton being inspired to write *Paradise Lost* or *Paradise Regained.* We are not talking about the same level of inspiration. This is the divine inspiration of God. The Bible claims that it is "God-breathed," *theopneustos.* It means more than just that God prompted the men to express things a certain way.

In the book of Genesis we read that God fashioned a man from the dust of the ground. After he had fashioned this man, he breathed into that man a living soul. It was the breath of God in a clay vessel that allowed that vessel to become a living soul. The Word of God has the same origin. God breathed into the Word of God, and it became the living Word, just as man became a living soul. The Bible is God-breathed.

"You know how, when you were a small child, you were taught the holy Scriptures; and it is these that make you wise to accept God's salvation by trusting Christ Jesus. The whole Bible was given to us by inspiration from God and is useful to teach us what is true and to make us realize what is wrong in our lives; it straightens us out and helps us to do what is right" (2 Tim. 3:15–16, TLB). This is the only time that the Greek word for *inspiration* is used. The writing is inspired, not the writer. The Scripture is given by inspiration of God, but the Scripture is the result of the breathing of God into the human vessel that recorded it. God was moving in holy men to record words that are divinely authoritative for our faith and practice.

When we want to know what we are to do, how we are to live, what we are to say, and how we are to act, we discover that by looking at the Word of God that was breathed out by God for us. "In telling you about these gifts we have even used the very words given to us by the Holy Spirit, not words that we as men might choose. So we use the Holy Spirit's words to explain the Holy Spirit's facts" (1 Cor. 2:13, TLB). The Bible is the spiritual product of the Holy Spirit of God.

What the Bible teaches is without error. Not everything the Bible contains is without error. There are some false sayings contained in the Bible, such as the false saying of the serpent when he told Eve that if she disobeyed God, God would not punish her, and she would not die as God had said (Gen. 3:4). That certainly is not the truth. The Bible contains false sayings of Satan. We need to be very careful as we study the Word of God to allow the Spirit of God to pinpoint for us the areas where false sayings and false prophets are quoted. However, what the Bible teaches is without error.

Inspiration refers to verbal inspiration. There are people who tell us today, "The thoughts are inspired, but not the words." How does one think without words? A thought is words that are unspoken. There is no way to accept that the Bible has certain great thoughts and principles that are inspired without also accepting that the words are inspired. We would be foolish indeed to make the Bible the basis for our study, our preaching, and our worship together if the words are not inspired. The Bible claims for itself verbal inspiration.

The Old Testament uses such phrases as "God said," "God spake," or "the word of the Lord came saying."

Jesus himself referred to this in Matthew 5:18: "For verily I say unto you, Till heaven and earth pass, one jot or one tittle shall in no wise pass from the law, till all be fulfilled." Verse 17 makes clear that the law refers to the entire Old Testament Scripture. It is all true. It is all valid. Not even a dot or a period is out of place. That is verbal inspiration. Every word, every grammatical phrasing is involved in inspiration.

The inspiration is plenary or complete. That simply means that there is not any part of Scripture that is without full doctrinal authority. Although I may not understand it, the Song of Solomon is just as much the Word of God as the Gospel of John. It is all fully and completely the Word of God. "It is easier for heaven and earth to pass, than one tittle of the law to fail" (Luke 16:17). Again, this is a reference to the Old Testament Scriptures in its totality. "These are the words which I spake unto you, while I was yet with you, that all things must be fulfilled, which were written in the law of Moses, and in the prophets, and in the psalms, concerning me" (Luke 24:44). The revelation of God in the Word of God is totally, fully, and completely authoritative. It is fully inspired.

The inspiration is varied. The writers all used their personalities and their unique style of writing. Just read the book of Hebrews and then read 1 John. There is a great deal of difference in the complexity of the language that is used. There is difference in styles and a variety of expressions, but the Bible is inspired by God. God had each one of these holy men say exactly what God wanted him to say, yet he used their own styles and personalities.

The Preserved Word

The Bible is the preserved word. This is important because when we talk about inspiration, obviously the thing that is

inspired is the original copy. In our contemporary transla-
tions we have access to much later manuscripts than did
those who translated the King James version in the latter
part of the sixteenth century and the early part of the seven-
teenth century. We now go back more nearly to the time
when the Bible was written. The miraculous thing is that
the more we discover of ancient manuscripts, the more we
discover that what we have is right. As far as the great eternal
truths of the Bible are concerned, we have not discovered
conflicts that alter the basic beliefs that we have. The Bible
is the preserved Word. The same God who inspired it and
revealed it has protected its transcription down to us.

The Imparted Word

It is one thing for the Holy Spirit to reveal to us the Word
of God, but it is another thing for us to appropriate the
truth of it. The Bible is the imparted word for those who
walk in the power of the Holy Spirit. The Holy Spirit gives
spiritual understanding to those who belong to him. "Oh,
there is so much more I want to tell you, but you can't
understand it now. All the Father's glory is mine; this is
what I mean when I say that he will show you my glory"
(John 16:12,15, TLB). The Holy Spirit will reveal to us that
which we need to know. In 1 Cor. 2:11–14 we have the
reminder that people who are not saved cannot appropriate
the Word of God because they do not have a spiritual disposi-
tion that allows God's Spirit freedom to work in their lives.

The Holy Spirit helps us to understand the Bible. This
understanding is for all of God's children. There are some
who think one has to be a seminary graduate or a Ph.D.
in order to understand the Bible. This is not true. "Knowing
this first, that no prophecy of the scripture is of any private
interpretation" (2 Pet. 1:20). That means that the proper
understanding of the Bible is no secret. God has revealed

unto us the deep things of his Word. The apostle Paul said, "Eye hath not seen, nor ear heard, neither have entered into the heart of man, the things which God hath prepared for them that love him. But God hath revealed them unto us by his Spirit" (1 Cor. 2:9–10).

The simplest saint, the most humble Christian can understand the tremendous eternal truths in the Word of God through the power of the Holy Spirit. We can ask God to bless us and impart to us an understanding of his Word. The Bible is for our reading, our study, and our edification. It is the Word of God hidden in our hearts that will protect us and keep us from sin. When we place God's Word in our hearts, he will impart to us spiritual and eternal truths.

One of the conditions for our receiving more understanding is for us to live the understanding we have. Jesus said, "If any man will do his will, he shall know of the doctrine, whether it be of God, or whether I speak of myself" (John 7:17). This is a valid principle: If any man shall *do* his will, he shall *know.* We do what we know to do, and God will give us deeper understanding. We must obey the imparted Word.

The United Word

Think with me a minute—sixty-six books, at least fifteen hundred years from the time the first one was written to the last one, forty different authors, several languages, hundreds of topics—and many of those who wrote did not have access to what the others had written. Yet the Bible is a united book. It is bound up in a common theme: the eternal purposes of God for the redemption of sinful man. We could put forty men in the same room today, tell them what we wanted them to say, and give them an outline; and they could not come up with anything that would have such unity.

Yet the Word of God was guided by the Holy Spirit of God over fifteen hundred years, through several languages, hundreds of topics, and nearly forty different people. It has a unity that is absolutely astonishing. One of the strongest arguments for the validity of the Scripture is its unity.

The Conclusive Word

The Bible is the conclusive Word of God. This is extremely important. "And I solemnly declare to everyone who reads this book: If anyone adds anything to what is written here, God shall add to him the plagues described in this book. And if anyone subtracts any part of these prophecies, God shall take away his share in the Tree of Life, and in the Holy City just described" (Rev. 22:18–19, TLB).

One may say, "That is talking about the book of Revelation." That is true. But we cannot write anything else without adding to it. It does not matter if that refers just to the book of Revelation or if it refers to all the inspired Word of God from Genesis to Revelation. There is nothing else to be added.

The Bible is the conclusive Word of God. Since that is true, everything we need is found in its pages. We simply need to diligently study and willingly obey what God has said. If someone says, "I have a new revelation from God," do not believe him. It is not so. The Bible has no new chapters. There are no addenda to it. Nothing new is to be added.

Every theological and moral dispute that we face has to be brought to the Word of God. That is where it is measured. Every experience we have is brought to the Word of God. We cannot measure truth by our experience. We measure our experience by the truth. Many false sayings are being passed off as spiritual truths. The Bible is the gauge. Check the sayings against the Bible.

It is time we quit debating it. We do not need to defend it. That is like trying to defend a lion against a cat. We do not need to do that. That lion can take care of itself. We do not need to defend the Bible; we need to expound it, believe it, and obey it. This is God's Word; and what God says, we are to do!

The Inerrant Word

The Bible is the inerrant word of God. Since it is divinely inspired, it is without error. The Bible is not a scientific textbook; but everywhere the Bible touches upon scientific fact, it is without error. It is not a history book; but all historical events recorded are true. Men have scoffed at the history of the Bible; yet every time an archaeologist turns his spade over, he verifies God's Word. Whatever God utters is true and without error.

The Transforming Word

There is one other thing that we must say about the Bible. It is the transforming Word of God. The greatest witness for the Word of God is what it does to us. "The Word of God is quick, and powerful, and sharper than any two-edged sword, piercing even to the dividing asunder of soul and spirit, and of the joints and marrow, and is a discerner of the thoughts and intents of the heart" (Heb. 4:12). The greatest testimony to the Word of God is that it transforms human life. Wherever the Word of God is read and proclaimed, comfort and strength is given to those who are bereaved; wisdom and guidance is distributed to those who are confused; those who are slaves to evil are liberated from their sins and evil habits, and their lives are transformed. Wherever the Word of God has touched, it has brought transformed lives.

That is not true of anything else. I read Bob Richards' book, *The Heart of a Champion*, but it did not change my life. I have read Dr. Kenneth Cooper's book on aerobics, but it did not change me. I read Norman Vincent Peale's *The Power of Positive Thinking*, but it did not change me. One day I read God's Word. The Holy Spirit took that Word and applied it to my heart. When he did, habits I could not break were broken. The apostle Peter said that we are born again by the Word of God (1 Pet. 1:23). There is no new birth apart from his Word. It is the transforming Word.

8
Satan

I am always hesitant to discuss Satan. He gets far more credit than he deserves. It is a great mistake for us to give Satan credit for many things. It pleases him to be discussed. By so doing we give him much more of a platform than he deserves. We blame many things on Satan that are nothing more than our sinful human natures. We are tempted when we are led astray by our own lusts (James 1:14). After our lust has led us astray, we are enticed, which is the work of Satan. But it is our lust that led us astray. There is much confusion and concern about Satan. We need to examine this doctrine carefully.

There is a devil. Throughout the Word of God there is reference to the nature, character, and work of Satan. Our personal experience verifies that truth. If we did not have the Word of God, we would know there is a devil because we have done business with him. We have met him, and we know that he is alive. He is the prince of this world, the one who influences for evil the affairs of this life. There will never be peace in the world because Satan dwells in the lives of most of the leaders of the world. We are in a world that is headed for destruction unless God intervenes.

In Isaiah 14 and Ezekiel 28 there is a description and reference to an earthy ruler. Yet beyond the description of the earthly ruler, there is an obvious reference to someone else. We see in these passages, beyond the historical settings, a description of the origin of Satan. "How you are fallen from heaven, O Lucifer, son of the morning! How you are cut down to the ground—mighty though you were against the nations of the world. For you said to yourself, I will ascend to heaven and rule the angels. I will take the highest throne. I will preside on the Mount of Assembly far away in the north. I will climb to the highest heavens and be like the Most High.' But instead, you will be brought down to the pit of hell, down to its lowest depths" (Isa. 14:12–15, TLB).

Satan was originally with God in God's heavenly host. He was a recognized and accepted part of God's creation and of God's angels. Because of pride in his heart, he was expelled from heaven. He assumed a position of dominance in this world.

The Origin of Satan

He was created as a beautiful angel of light. He was called Lucifer. He was a perfect creation of God. He was the fairest of all God's creation. "You were the perfection of wisdom and beauty. You were perfect in all you did from the day you were created until that time when wrong was found in you. Your heart was filled with pride because of all your beauty; you corrupted your wisdom for the sake of your splendor" (Ezek. 28:12,15,17, TLB). He was perfect in the eyes of God in his beauty and in his wisdom.

Yet out of this came pride that caused him to stumble. If we can understand what happened to Satan, we can understand what causes us to stumble many times. For "pride goeth before destruction" (Prov. 16:18). The middle letter in *pride* is the same middle letter as in *sin*. It is *I*. Read again carefully Isaiah 14 and note that at least five times in the framework of a few sentences, Satan says, "I will do this," "I will do that," etc. Because of an unconquered pride, because of an undisciplined pride, because of an unyielded pride, a desire welled up in his heart for him to be more powerful than God. He was not content with his authority and power. He wanted to be God. That is the essence of all sin—for us to be discontent with what we have, what we are, and what God has placed in our lives—and to seek to gain something that is beyond what has been placed in our hands.

"Thou art the anointed cherub that covereth; and I have set thee so" (Ezek. 28:14). God gave Satan the responsibility of covering the very throne of God. Instead of covering the throne of God, he coveted the throne of God. He wanted that throne. His pride led him to rebel against God. The Bible is not precise at the point of Satan's entry into the world. We do know that he was created perfect and beautiful. Yet in rebellion against God, he fell from a state of perfection and was cast into this world. Thus, this world is his domain.

He was the original sinner. He was a sinner from the beginning (1 John 3:8). He was the first one to rebel against God and has led that rebellion ever since.

The Nature of Satan

Satan is not simply a force of evil or an evil influence. He is a real person. He is spoken of as a person. He is dealt with as a person. He is characterized as a person. We are dealing with a real person, not an impersonal force.

He is called by many names and titles. He is called Lucifer, the devil, Satan, Beelzebub, Belial, Adversary, Dragon, Serpent, god of the world, prince of this world, the prince of the power of the air. He is the accuser of the brethren, the enemy, the tempter, the wicked one, the fouler, the wolf, the destroyer, a roaring lion, a thief, the father of lies, a murderer, the sower of discord. All of those are fearful titles. Each one of them gives us insight into the character and nature of Satan.

He is a presumptuous person. He presumes upon his authority and power. His presumptuous nature is seen in the first chapter of Job. There we see him presumptuously confronting God concerning Job. He is wicked and evil by nature (1 John 2:13). He is supremely subtle (Gen. 3:1). He is able to call black white and make us believe it. He is a powerful person (Eph. 2:2). He is, by nature, unmerciful. Luke 9 reveals the story of the inhabiting of an individual by the cohorts of Satan. The description there is one of terror that resided in the heart and of the tragedy that existed because of their presence. The individual was driven, beaten, and hounded. When we follow the tracks of Satan, we discover that he is unmerciful. Kindness, love, and compassion have never been attributes of Satan. He is an unmerciful adversary. He is called "a roaring lion . . . seeking whom he may devour" (1 Pet. 5:8). He unmercifully wants to hurt and to destroy our happiness. He wants to make it impossible for us to ever have peace and fulfillment. We ought to be suspicious of every word that Satan whispers to us. Behind every contact is an unmerciful drive to destroy everything that we have.

He is the great pretender. He is not what he seems to be. Notice that he goes about "as a roaring lion" (1 Pet. 5:8). He is an imitation. He is a fake. He is a paper lion. He pretends to be something that he is not. That is his nature. He is pretentious and hypocritical.

He is not omnipotent. He is limited. He is more powerful than we are, but he is not all-powerful. He is not omnipresent. He can move faster than we can, but he cannot be everywhere at once. He is not omniscient. He is smarter than we are, but he does not know everything. He is limited by his nature as a person. God has placed this limitation on him. When he fell from the glories of heaven, he did not bring with him the all-knowing mind of God.

The Activities of Satan

He is a sinner from the beginning (1 John 3:8). He is the essence of sin. He rebels against the will and the purposes of God. He wants to destory everything that is godly, everything that is right. He has great pride. He is condemned for the pride in his heart (1 Tim. 3:6). Although he cannot be everywhere at once, he goes from place to place. He has many associates and many partners who help spread his evil about.

The chief exercise of his authority is in this world (Eph. 2:2). He is head of the powers of darkness (Eph. 6:10–18). That does not mean that he has unbridled control of this world. According to 2 Thessalonians 2:7,8 the Holy Spirit restrains him. Satan is the prince of this world. He is the head of the powers of darkness, but he operates within the restrictions of the sovereignty of God. Read again carefully the book of Job to see the extent to which God sometimes allows Satan to go. Numerous verses tell us of his control over fallen angels. He has many demons with which to work.

He is active in religious affairs (2 Cor. 11:14). The devil is a very religious person. If we think that he is not, we are sadly mistaken. Many times we have the concept that he is an atheist. No sir! Satan knows there is a God. Satan is no atheist at all. He is very active in religious affairs, and that is why we find some of the most ungodly things in the framework of churches. Satan attends church quite often.

He is the author of persecution and tribulation. All of the distresses that come upon us as individuals find their source in Satan. He attacks us with cunning snares and fiery darts (Eph. 6:16). Satan is a very active person.

The Fate of Satan

He is a defeated foe. His death warrant was signed on Calvary's cross. When Jesus Christ died, was buried, and was raised from the dead, he had in his hand the keys of death and hell. There was therein the death certificate for Satan. His fate is certain. Jesus Christ lived, died on the cross, and was raised in order that he might defeat him who has the power of death, the devil (Heb. 2:14). Satan has been defeated. His power has been broken. He will share eternal doom with those he has seduced. That is why Satan is so active now. He knows his time is limited (Rev. 12:12). He knows that now is the time God is giving for people to be saved (2 Pet. 3:9). During this time, Satan is working busily because he knows his fate is sealed. When Jesus Christ returns to earth with his saints, he will sentence Satan, and his judgment will be secure.

The Conquest of Satan

How do we conquer Satan? How do we deal with him? We are to deal with him in Christ's name. There will never come a time when we can deal with Satan in our own strength. We must always face Satan in Christ's name. Ephesians 1:19–22 speaks of the power and the authority that is vested in the presence of Christ and in the name of Christ. It is in his name that we must always approach Satan.

I am very suspicious of people who are always casting

Satan out of places and people. None of us can begin to be careless in dealing with Satan. That is the responsibility of Jesus. We need to be very sure that when we rebuke or deal with Satan in any way, it is always in Jesus' name. It is always serious business to encounter Satan.

We are to "Be sober, be vigilant; because your adversary the devil, as a roaring lion, walketh about, seeking whom he may devour: Whom resist stedfast in the faith" (1 Pet. 5:8,9). We are to be watching, to be disciplined, and to be alert for his attack. It is most dangerous for us to get careless. When we least expect it, Satan strikes us. Carelessness is always dangerous. When we get careless, we make mistakes in what we are doing. When we get careless about driving a car, we have an accident. When we get careless about balancing the books, we make mistakes. We must be serious in this matter of dealing with Satan.

We are not to give him any place in our lives (Eph. 4:27). We are not to give him a place in our habits. We are not to give him a place in our attitudes and activities. He is to have no place in our words. Sometimes we think a matter is unimportant. That is not so. Every matter is significant with Satan. Give him a foothold, and he will tear our lives apart and destroy us.

Many of the problems we face today are results of our carelessness in dealing with the devil. When our children go wrong, chances are there was a time when we gave place to Satan in our lives by not having the kind of discipline or the kind of love, compassion, and communication that we ought to have. When we have problems, it is because there was a time when we gave Satan a foothold. He just needs a little bit. When we have problems at business, at home, or at church, it is because we have given him a place in our lives. We must not do so.

We cannot control our husbands or our wives, our fathers or our mothers, our sisters or our brothers, our sons or our daughters, or our friends. We only have some control over ourselves. So we must not give him a place in our lives. As we do that collectively, we will not give him a place in our fellowship. If we are to conquer him, there must not be a place for him in our lives.

As we approach Satan, we are to put on the whole armor of God (Eph. 6). That reminds us that we are in a fight. We are to put on the whole armor of God that we may be able to stand against the craftiness of the devil. Why is that so?

"We wrestle not against flesh and blood, but against principalities, against powers, against the rulers of the darkness of this world, against spiritual wickedness in high places. Wherefore take unto you the whole armour of God, that ye may be able to withstand in the evil day, and having done all, to stand. Stand therefore, having your loins girt about with truth, and having on the breastplate of righteousness; And your feet shod with the preparation of the gospel of peace; Above all, taking the shield of faith, wherewith ye shall be able to quench all the fiery darts of the wicked. And take the helmet of salvation, and the sword of the Spirit, which is the word of God" (Eph. 6:12–17). When we put on God's armor, Satan will have no victory over us.

We are not to be ignorant of his craftiness and his devices (2 Cor. 2:11). Ultimately we overcome Satan by the Word of God. That is how Jesus did it. Jesus overcame him by the Word. Three times he was tempted, and each time Jesus answered, "It is written." The apostle John said, "I have written unto you, fathers, because ye have known him that is from the beginning. I have written unto you, young men, because ye are strong, and the word of God abideth in you, and ye have overcome the wicked one" (1 John 2:14).

He is overcome by the Word of God abiding within. That is why when we gather and the preacher stands to preach, he ought to preach the Word of God. That is why when we gather in Sunday School to study, we ought to study the Word of God. That is why the Word of God is the most significant pursuit of or lives. The Bible declares, "Thy word have I hid in my heart, that I might not sin against thee" (Ps. 119:11).

The devil is the original sinner. He is the source of all sinfulness in the world. If we are to conquer him, we must take the Word of God and place it in our hearts. Through his Word and the power of his Holy Spirit, God will give us victory. Satan is a powerful adversary. He is the enemy of all that is good and wholesome, but he is a defeated foe. We do not need to be frightened by him, for we face him in the strength of One who has already defeated Satan. His fate is secured and determined because Jesus Christ has risen victorious from the grave and holds in his hand the death sentence of Satan. Thus it is important for us to stand in the power of God.

There are some things we can do. We are to be alert. We are to be vigilant, always on the lookout. We are to give Satan no place in our lives. We are to put on the whole armor of God. By his Word, victory will be ours.

9
The Church

People have many different ideas concerning the nature and purpose of the church. It is vital for us to discover the scriptural teaching concerning the church.

"Then they that gladly received his word were baptized; and the same day there were added unto them about three thousand souls. And they continued stedfastly in the apostles' doctrine and fellowship, and in breaking of bread, and in prayers. And fear came upon every soul: and many wonders and signs were done by the apostles. And all that believed were together, and had all things common; and sold their possessions and goods, and parted them to all men, as every man had need. And they, continuing daily with one accord in the temple, and breaking bread from house to house, did eat their meat with gladness and singleness of heart, Praising God, and having favour with all the people. And the Lord added to the church daily such as should be saved" (Acts 2:41–47).

"And now beware! Be sure you feed and shepherd God's flock—his church, purchased with his blood—for the Holy Spirit is holding you responsible as overseers" (Acts 20:28, TLB).

"God has put all things under his feet and made him the supreme Head of the church—which is his body, filled with himself, the Author and Giver of everything everywhere" (Eph. 1:22–23, TLB).

"And you husbands, show the same kind of love to your wives as Christ showed to the church when he died for her" (Eph. 5:25, TLB).

"And he is the head of the body, the church: who is the beginning, the firstborn from the dead; that in all things he might have the preeminence" (Col. 1:18).

And in response to the question of Jesus, "Whom do men say that I the Son of man am? . . . Simon Peter answered and said, Thou art the Christ, the Son of the living God. And Jesus answered and said unto him, Blessed art thou, Simon Barjona: for flesh and blood hath not revealed it unto thee, but my Father which is in heaven. And I say also unto thee, That thou art Peter, and upon this rock I will build my church; and the gates of hell shall not prevail against it' " (Matt. 16:13,16–18).

There are many other verses relating to the doctrine of the church. In the Old Testament the Hebrew word which corresponds to the Greek word *ecclesia* in the New Testament appears more than 120 times. The Greek word *ecclesia* appears 114 times in the New Testament.

The Nature of the Church

We need to examine carefully the word that is translated "church" in our English Bible. It is the Greek word *ecclesia*. *Ek* means out of and *kaleo* means to call. Literally the word means the called out ones. The church is composed of called out ones. The very nature of the word indicates that not everybody is in the church. If they were, there would not be anybody to be called out from. The primary usage of the word in the New Testament is that which refers to a group of believers who had been called out of the pursuits

of the world and into the heart of God, to be used for his
purposes.

There was a group around the Lord Jesus prior to the
day of Pentecost, but the most sound reasoning would indicate that the church, as we understand it, originated on
the day of Pentecost, in the coming to power of the Holy
Spirit of God.

Our English word *church* actually comes from a Greek
word *kuriakon*, which means belonging to God or the house
of God. We have a dual meaning, for the church is not a
building. There were no church buildings in the New Testament. Only after the apostolic age were church buildings
as such built. Never does the word *church* in the New Testament refer to a building.

We have almost completely made the building the meaning of the word. "That is our church," we say, and we point
to the building. "Where is your church located?" we ask.
We have made the word *church* to refer primarily to a building of brick and mortar. This is not the case in the Bible.
The church is not the building. The church meets in the
building. *We* are the church. The church is comprised of
living stones. The very word *church* indicates that people
comprise, in themselves, a building for God to inhabit. The
New Testament speaks of the Holy Spirit coming and dwelling in our hearts. As the Holy Spirit dwells within us, we
become the dwelling place of the Holy Spirit.

In its New Testament usage, at least 99 of the 114 times,
ecclesia refers to a local body of believers. There are many
people who say that they do not need the local church. That
is a violation of the Scripture. If it were not for the local
church, there would be no New Testament. The New Testament was largely written to the local church. There is a
visible church in our community, and we are to be part of

that church. It is comforting to know that there are Christians in Germany, Argentina, Japan, Canada, Florida, and California. But that does not strengthen my faith or build up my spirit. Those of us in the local church grow and mature because we work and worship together through our local assembly. We will not understand the true nature of the church unless we see it as a local body of believers. Several times the New Testament speaks of "the church in their house" or "the church which meets in your home." Since there was no church building, the house became the focal point for many of the local churches.

Ecclesia is also used occasionally in the New Testament to refer to the whole body of believers. The universal church finds its real meaning for us, however, through the local church. Some people say, "I belong to the invisible, universal church. I do not believe in the local church." That is false reasoning. That would be like saying that one belongs to mankind but was not born to parents first. We have local expressions of our being. As we grow in an understanding of what it means to relate to one father and one mother, one home and one community, we are able to understand that we are a part of mankind in its great universal sense. Just as we need that local experience in the home in order to grasp and understand our place in mankind, so we need the local church to understand our place in the universal church.

The church is founded upon the principle of the deity of Jesus Christ. Jesus asked, "Whom do men say that I . . . am?" The disciples gave him some answers that were circulating around Galilee at the time. Then he asked, "Whom say ye that I am?" Simon Peter spoke up immediately and said, "Thou art the Christ, the Son of the living God." Jesus said, "Blessed art thou, Simon Barjona: for flesh and blood hath not revealed it unto thee, but my Father which is in Heaven. And I say also unto thee, That thou art Peter, and upon this rock I will build my church" (Matt. 16:13–18).

Many have said that the church is built upon Peter. That is not so. The word for rock as ascribed to Peter and the word that is translated rock, upon which Jesus built the church, are not the same word in the original language. He was saying, "You are Peter, a stone, and upon this rock, upon this gigantic boulder, I will build my church." The church was to be built upon the confession of the deity of Christ. If one denies the deity of Christ, he cannot be a part of the true church. The church is not a social agency for the purpose of reformation of mankind. It is not simply a place to get together. It is a fellowship in which we worship based upon the eternal truth that Jesus is the Christ, the Son of the living God.

The church is an organism. It is an organization. As an organism it is growing, maturing, ever changing, and enlarging in its relationships. As an organization, it is assigned a task to perform, ordinances to administer, and a mission to achieve and accomplish. It is both an organism and an organization. That is the nature of the church.

The Members of the Church

The Bible tells us that a church member is a regenerated believer. The true church member has been born again and is to be a baptized believer. Immediately one asks, "Do you have to be baptized to be saved?" No—the thief on the cross was not baptized, yet he was saved. Some might say, "That is an exception." However, there are no exceptions to God's absolute laws. If baptism were essential for salvation, then Jesus would have made sure that the man on the cross was baptized. Baptism is our public break with the world.

It is the public expression of our commitment to Jesus Christ. None of us is meant to live under water. If we stay too long, we drown.

The word *baptizo* in the Greek language was used to refer to immersion. When someone drowned, the Greeks said they were baptized to death. Baptism cannot be anything but immersion. Sprinkling or pouring could not possibly drown anybody. When we are placed under water, we are putting our bodies in a position of death and are symbolizing death to an old life and resurrection to a new life. The local church is comprised of born-again believers who have been baptized.

The New Testament further indicates that the local church is comprised of loving and united believers. God's intention is for the church members to love each other. We are to be loving and compassionate. "Be ye kind one to another, tenderhearted, forgiving one another" (Eph. 4:32). On the day of Pentecost, the Christians were all in one place with one accord, and they continued united in purpose and practice. The real church is comprised of people who, though diverse and different, are united in love. There are many chronic complainers who are not part of the church. If one finds himself always complaining and critical, he had better look seriously at his faith. There is no excuse for divisiveness in God's church. The members of the church are born again, baptized, and filled with love and unity of purpose.

The Government of the Church

There are several things that are significant concerning the government of the church. First of all, the Bible clearly indicates that the local church is an autonomous body. Nobody dictates to the local church. We are at complete liberty to determine the direction and destiny of our local church. We are almost unique in this. Most of the major religious denominations across the world are organized from the top down. They have a system of hierarchy, a level of command. Someone is in command at each of the levels, and the local church is ultimately instructed what to do. That is not true in Baptist life. We have always maintained the priesthood of the believer and the autonomy of the local church. The church is autonomous and self-governing.

Secondly, the New Testament church is a theocratic democracy. There is a freedom within the church for the membership to express itself. Each member is called upon many times to express prayerful decisions and commitments. There are those who would have us believe that the church is an absolute perfect democracy. Well, it is not. No one tells the pastor what to preach; yet the church hears him approximately 150 times each year. So it is not a democracy when it comes to the preaching. God tells the pastor what to preach. It is not necessarily a democracy when it comes to many of the details of the program and ministry of the church. We have general guidelines that the church has adopted, but there is a great deal of freedom, yet restriction, within the democracy.

The church is a theocratic democracy. That simply means that our freedom as individuals within the church springs from our obedience to Christ. Our democracy is based upon biblical principles. We have no right to vote whether or not to do something that God has already told us to do. If the Bible tells us to do something, we do not need to vote on it. If the Bible tells us to win the lost, baptize, and teach them, we do not have to vote every week on whether we are going to win the lost, baptize, and teach them. We have already been instructed to do that. There is liberty and freedom within the framework of the lordship of Jesus Christ and his Word in our lives.

The church is a theocratic democracy based upon the principles of the Word of God. It is probably better understood to say that the church is a theocracy or Christocracy that has many democratic principles. Our freedom springs from the fact that we have given complete obedience to Jesus Christ and to his Word.

One other thing about the government of the church ought to be said. The Bible indicates the absolute separation of church and state. The separation of church and state means that the church does not tell the state how to run the government, and the government does not tell the church how to run the church. Obviously, there is going to be some contact. We have a responsibility as Christians to be the very best citizens in the land. The reason is simple. Whatever authority exists does so because God has ordained it. Christians ought to be involved in the processes of democracy. But as far as the government's dictating to us, God does not intend for it to be so. As far as the church trying to dictate to the government, the Bible indicates a complete separation of church and state.

The Ordinances of the Church

There are two ordinances that God has given to the church as outward expressions of our mission. The ordinances are baptism and the Lord's Supper. Baptism tells the story of our salvation. It tells the story of death to an old way of life and resurrection to a new way of life. Baptism is our way of breaking with the old world and stepping forth into a new life-style under God. The Lord's Supper is a succinct statement of our faith and doctrine. The Christ who saved

us is going to come back again. The Lord's Supper is a reminder of what he has done and what he is going to do. It
is a memorial of his death in the past, and it is a reminder
that he is coming again in the future. He said, "As often
as ye eat this bread, and drink this cup ye do shew the
Lord's death till he come" (1 Cor. 11:26). The Lord's Supper
is given to the church as an expression of our faith in the
finished, redemptive purposes of Jesus Christ and the ultimate return of Christ to fulfill the promises he has given
to us in the Bible.

In the New Testament only those who were baptized
participated in the Lord's Supper. The Lord's Supper is intended to be observed only by those who have been scrip-
turally immersed following their personal faith and commitment to the Lord Jesus Christ as a symbol and sign of their
faith in him.

The Mission of the Church

There are at least three basic purposes for the church.
No true church neglects any one of these facets.

The first mission is to provide spiritual growth for the
membership. Jesus commanded the church to "Go ye therefore, and teach all nations, baptizing them in the name of
the Father, and of the Son, and of the Holy Ghost: Teaching
them to observe all things whatsoever I have commanded
you: and, lo, I am with you alway, even unto the end of
the world" (Matt. 28:19–20). Any church that does not do
this as a means of encouraging spiritual maturity and growth
is failing in its basic mission.

None of us has achieved perfection. We are still growing
and learning. The church needs to be an incubator in which
we can grow, mature, and enlarge our faith. It is to be a
place where we can have our lives challenged, where we

can have our sins convicted, and where we can commit ourselves afresh to Christ.

Secondly, the church has a mission of propagating the gospel around the world. That is why we give ourselves and our money to missions. Some people say, "Why, there are plenty of lost people here." That is true. But God, who has called us together, has said, "This gospel of the kingdom shall be preached in all the world for a witness unto all nations; and then shall the end come" (Matt. 24:14).

There is a worldwide obligation that rests upon the church. We are to propagate the gospel from here and on to the ends of the earth. That is why persecution came to the early church. In the book of Acts we find the church just gathering. The church at Jerusalem had many thousands of members. They would have stayed there and built a shrine. However, they became the object of persecution, and they were scattered abroad. The book of Acts said that "they that were scattered abroad went every where preaching the word." (Acts 8:4). That is the mission of the church.

The third mission really includes the first two—the mission of proclaiming the Word of God. We are to teach and preach the Word of God. Whatever we do and say should be based upon the Word of God. No one else is going to preach it. No one else is going to teach it. Someone else will feed the poor. Someone else will clothe the poor. Someone else will teach the illiterate to read. Someone else will minister to the handicapped. Our unique task is to preach the gospel.

Do not misunderstand. We should feed the poor and so on. But, without apology, what we do in a social vein is always for the purpose of teaching and preaching the Word of God. Any social action by the church that does not teach or preach the Word of God is not Christian missions; it is simply social concern. We are to preach the Word to others as we care for their needs.

One other thing ought to be said about the church. Jesus said that "the gates of hell shall not prevail against it" (Matt. 16:18). Most people have taken that to mean that the church is built like a mighty fortress, and Satan and the gates of hell are pounding on the door of the church but cannot knock it down. Read it again. "Upon this rock I will build my church; and the gates of hell shall not prevail [shall not stand up] against it." It is not that hell is assaulting the church and the church will withstand. Rather, the church is assaulting hell, and hell will not stand against the church.

The church is not a passive, milquetoast organization to be tossed about by the whims of a pagan world. But the church is a militant, aggressive army, marching against the enemy. God has assigned us to march on the gates of hell, and he has promised us victory. The battle is won. The victory is ours. Claim it! March on, church of God, march on! The gates of hell will fall before you. That is the church. Militant! Aggressive! Victorious!

10
Our Eternal Home

Many times we claim a belief in heaven; then when someone dies, we act as though it were a myth. We carry on as though all we say we believe is not true.

God has given to us beautiful truths about heaven. The apostle Paul said, "I would not have you to . . . sorrow . . . as others which have no hope" (1 Thess. 4:13). He was not saying that we should not sorrow because sorrow is the result of the way God made us emotionally. We grieve when someone we love is removed from us by death. But we are not to grieve or sorrow hopelessly. God has prepared adequately and wondrously for us. "For we know that if our earthly house of this tabernacle were dissolved, we have a building of God, an house not made with hands, eternal in the heavens" (2 Cor. 5:1). There are three basic things that the Bible tells us about heaven.

A Perfect Place

The Bible tells us that heaven is a perfect place. "Let not your heart be troubled: ye believe in God, believe also in me. In my Father's house are many mansions: if it were not so, I would have told you. I go to prepare a place for you. And if I go and prepare a place for you, I will come again, and receive you unto myself; that where I am, there ye may be also" (John 14:1–3). Twice in these verses, Jesus called heaven a place. It is not a myth. It is not a state of mind. It is not an emotion. It is a very real place for us to live, and it is a perfect place.

The list of perfections are quite impressive. It is a place of perfect beauty. "And the building of the wall of it was of jasper: and the city was pure gold, like unto clear glass. And the foundations of the wall of the city were garnished with all manner of precious stones. And the twelve gates were twelve pearls; every several gate was of one pearl: and the street of the city was pure gold, as it were transparent glass" (Rev. 21:18–19,21). As we read of heaven, we discover indescribable beauty. Imagine a pearl big enough to be a gate. Imagine gold so crystal clear and so abundant that it becomes something to walk upon. Imagine the foundations of the city with diamonds and rubies and precious stones. When God revealed to us the beauties of heaven, he described a place of perfect beauty.

It is a place of perfect fellowship with God. Jesus said, "I go to prepare a place for you . . . that where I am, there ye may be also" (John 14:3). In the heart of every child of God is a desire to have fellowship with him. Whatever desire exists in the hearts of God's children is perfectly supplied in heaven. It is a place of perfect fellowship with God.

It is a place of perfect fellowship with others. "I saw a new heaven and a new earth: for the first heaven and the first earth were passed away; and there was no more sea" (Rev. 21:1). The apostle John wrote this while marooned on the isle of Patmos. Every day as he rose to greet the new day, he saw a sea that separated him from those he loved. When God allowed him to glimpse inside heaven, the first thing he noticed was that there was no sea. There was nothing to separate, nothing to keep him away from those he loved. It was a perfect place of fellowship with others. The apostle Paul said concerning the coming again of the Lord: "The dead in Christ shall rise first: Then we which are alive and remain shall be caught up together with them in the clouds, to meet the Lord in the air: and so shall we ever be with the Lord" (1 Thess. 4:16–17). We shall be with him and with each other.

It is a place of perfect understanding. There are many things we do not know now. There are many things we cannot comprehend. Our wisdom is too weak and halting for us to fathom the meaning of many experiences. But in heaven there will be perfect understanding. The apostle Paul said, "Now we see through a glass, darkly; but then face to face: now I know in part; but then shall I know even as also I am known" (1 Cor. 13:12). It is vague here. The pictures that we see are not clearly defined or distinct. All of the whys we have asked and all of the things we have failed to comprehend will be perfectly understood when we stand in God's perfect heaven.

It is a place of perfect provision. Jesus said to John, "I am Alpha and Omega, the beginning and the end. I will give unto him that is athirst of the fountain of the water of life freely" (Rev. 21:6). Jesus is the beginning and the end, and he is everything in between. Everything we need from the first experience of our lives to the last experience is provided. The place he has prepared for us is a place of perfect provision.

It is a place of abundance (Rev. 22:1–6). There are no beggars in heaven. There are no people walking down the street wanting something they do not have. There are no people who have desires that have not found fulfillment. There is no want, no poverty there. There is nothing that would physically or spiritually cause a famished spirit. Heaven is a place of perfect provision for our needs.

Further, we find that it is a place of perfect comfort. "God shall wipe away all tears from their eyes; and there shall be no more death, neither sorrow, nor crying, neither shall there be any more pain: for the former things are passed away" (Rev. 21:4). There will be no pain to cause grief or sadness. There will be no death to cause tears to flow freely. Every cause for tears and grief will have been removed. It is a place of perfect comfort.

Earthly comfort is temporary. When another grief comes to our hearts, we need to be comforted again. In heaven, God shall wipe away the tears, and they are wiped away forever. God shall remove death, and it will never again come into our experience. God shall remove every cause of grief and every cause of sorrow. The comfort of heaven is perfect. It never has to be repeated.

More than that, the Bible tells us that heaven is a place of perfect rest. "Blessed are the dead which die in the Lord from henceforth: Yea, saith the Spirit, that they may rest from their labours" (Rev. 14:13). All weariness will be gone. We all understand weariness. We live at such a pace that weariness is a constant problem with us. Perfect rest is ours in heaven. There will be no weariness there. No tired feet there! No bloodshot eyes there! Perfect rest! That for which our bodies and souls long will be ours. There is the need for physical rest. There is also the need for emotional and mental rest. All of that is perfectly provided for in heaven.

It will also be a place of perfect holiness. Everyone of us wants to be better than we are. We do not like the imperfections we see in ourselves. It grieves our hearts that they are there. But in heaven, that wish will be transferred into reality, and we will be perfectly holy. "There shall in no wise enter into it any thing that defileth, neither whatsoever worketh abomination, or maketh a lie: but they which are written in the Lamb's book of life. There shall be no more curse" (Rev. 21:27; 22:3). There will be no sin there. There will be nothing ungodly there.

It is a place of perfect joy. God will wipe away all tears and remove all the causes for grief and sadness. When he removes the things which cause grief, then the joy which is put in its place is a perfect joy!

Heaven will be a place of perfect service. "Therefore are they before the throne of God, and serve him day and night in his temple: and he that sitteth on the throne shall dwell among them" (Rev. 7:15). That is one of the most beautiful thoughts our minds could ever grasp. God sits on the throne, yet he dwells among them. He who is on the throne is just as close to the person in the last row as he is the one on the front row. He dwells in their midst. When we walk in that kind of relationship with him, service is a delight. It is perfect service when we serve in his presence and in his power. "There shall be no more curse: but the throne of God and of the Lamb shall be in it; and his servants shall serve him" (Rev. 22:3)

Here we offer imperfect service in our own strength. When we lift up our abilities, our strength, it is incomplete. Our service is not what it ought to be. But in heaven, it will be perfect service.

It is a place of perfect light. There is no night there. There is no darkness. "The city had no need of sun or moon to light it, for the glory of God and of the Lamb illuminate it. Its light will light the nations of the earth, and the rulers of the world will come an bring their glory to it. And there will be no night there—no need for lamps or sun—for the Lord God will be their light; and they shall reign forever and ever" (Rev. 21:23, 24; 22:5, TLB). Everything we fear comes shrouded in darkness. We are afraid of the night.

We associate darkness with that which is forbidding and that which is frightening. When we look at heaven, we find a place of perfect light. There is no need for the sun and the moon, for God is the light and the glory of it all.

It is a place of perfect glory. After the apostle Paul said that we are "troubled on every side, yet not distressed; we are perplexed, yet not in despair; Persecuted, but not forsaken; cast down, but not destroyed" he said, "For our light affliction, which is but for a moment, worketh for us a far more exceeding and external weight of glory" (2 Cor. 4:8, 9,17). We experience perfect glory, his glory. It is his power, his presence in us. "When Christ, who is our life, shall appear, then shall ye also appear with him in glory" (Col. 3:4). It is a place of perfect glory.

It is a place of perfect worship. "After this I saw a vast crowd, too great to count, from all nations and provinces and languages, standing in front of the throne and before the Lamb, clothed in white, with palm branches in their hands. And they were shouting with a mighty shout, 'Salvation comes from our God upon the throne, and from the Lamb.' And now all the angels were crowding around the throne and around the Elders and the four Living Beings, and falling face down before the throne and worshiping God. 'Amen!' they said. 'Blessing, and glory, and wisdom, and thanksgiving, and honor, and power, and might, be to our God forever and forever. Amen!'" (Rev. 7:9–12, TLB). Often we have the experience of wanting to love God more than we do and wanting to adore him more that we do. In heaven we will realize that desire.

A Prepared Place

It is a perfect place, but it is also a prepared place. First of all, it is prepared for God. Only a place such as we have described is a fit place for God. God has to have a place of perfection. The throne is his. The city is his. It is his heaven that we are talking about. Heaven is a prepared place for God.

But it is also a prepared place for God's children. God has prepared it for us. Jesus said, "I go to prepare a place for you" (John 14:2). It is prepared for those who have given their hearts to Jesus Christ. Jesus Christ died in order that he might open the way into heaven. He rose again so that he might demonstrate that he possessed the power to bring forgiveness for our sins and to free us from the chains that bind us. He is now preparing a place for those who have given themselves in faith to him. Heaven is a prepared place for a prepared people.

Many people believe that we may travel different paths to heaven. They believe that there are different ways of getting into heaven. But the Bible says, "there is none other name under heaven given among men, whereby we must be saved" (Acts 4:12). "I am the way, the truth, and the life: no man cometh unto the Father, but by me" (John 14:6). There is only one way to heaven. That way is Jesus Christ. We must be prepared through personal faith in him to enter that place which has been prepared for God's children.

A Personal Place

It is a personal place. Many people wonder if we will know each other over there. The Scripture is clear concerning this.

"But some man will say, How are the dead raised up? and with what body do they come? Thou fool, that which thou sowest is not quickened, except it die: And that which thou sowest, thou sowest not that body that shall be, but bare grain, it may chance of wheat, or of some other grain: But God giveth it a body as it hath pleased him, and to every seed his own body. All flesh is not the same flesh: but there is one kind of flesh of men, another flesh of beasts, another of fishes, and another of birds. There are also celestial bodies, and bodies terrestrial: but the glory of the celestial is one, and the glory terrestrial is another. There is one glory of the sun, and another glory of the moon, and another glory of the stars: for one star differeth from another star in glory. So also is the resurrection of the dead. It is sown in corruption; it is raised in incorruption: It is sown in dishonour; it is raised in glory: it is sown in weakness; it is raised in power: it is sown a natural body; it is raised a spiritual body. There is a natural body, and there is a spiritual body. Now this I say, brethren, that flesh and blood cannot inherit the kingdom of God; neither doth corruption inherit incorruption. Behold, I shew you a mystery: We shall not all sleep, but we shall all be changed, In a moment, in the twinkling of an eye, at the last trump: for the trumpet shall sound, and the dead shall be raised incorruptible, and we shall be changed. For this corruptible must put on incorruption, and this mortal must put on immortality. . . .then shall be brought to pass the saying that is written, Death is swallowed up in victory. O death, where is thy sting? O grave, where is thy victory? The sting of death is sin; and the strength of sin is the law. But thanks be to God, which giveth us the victory through our Lord Jesus Christ" (1 Cor. 15:35–44, 50–57).

This passage reveals three very simple things. First, it tells us that we will still have distinct personalities. We will know each other. Do we think that we would know less over there than we know here? We will have individual glorified bodies. Our bodies will have the same basic characteristics of our

Lord Jesus Christ. They will be eternal. They will be immortal. Yet each will be distinct and known individually.

Often people say, "When I get to heaven, I am going to talk to Noah about the flood. I am going to talk to Paul about the missionary journeys. I am going to talk to John about when he went into the heaven of heavens, and God gave him the beautiful vision of heaven. I am going to talk to Moses about the Red Sea," and so on. If we only think of heaven as a place of great beauty, of wonderful, perfect provision, and of fellowship with each other, we will miss the whole point of what God says about heaven. Our occupation in heaven will not be with our position, our privileges, or with our glory, but with our Lord.

The important thing is that we are going to be with him. We are going to worship the Lord. We are going to love the Lord. Every human attachment we have had, whether it be husband or wife, father or mother, or son or daughter, will fade into insignificance. The focal point of heaven is God. Over and again in Revelation is the refrain, "Worthy is the Lamb"—references to his glory and his person abound.

We have had people love us, but no one has ever loved us as Jesus had. When we stand in his heaven, that place he has prepared, our concern will not be to see Mother or Father, husband or wife, a saint of by-gone days, or a hero for the pages of the Bible. Our concern in that moment of perfect immortality, with the capacity to understand what God's wonderful plan and purpose has been all through the ages, will be turned toward him. No one ever loved us as he does! No one ever suffered for us as he did! No one ever provided for us as he has! We will worship and love him eternally in heaven.

11

The Reality of Hell

There is nothing that would quicken us to loyalty and to devoted service more than an understanding of hell. Nothing would drive a sinner to God faster than if that sinner could see his ultimate destiny in hell. The doctrine of hell is consistent with the judgment and the justice of God.

The reality of hell is one of the dominant notes in the Word of God. There is more about hell that there is about heaven. There is another side of God that we need to look at: "The Lord is known by the judgment which he executeth: the wicked is snared in the work of his own hands. . . . The wicked shall be turned into hell, and all the nations that forget God" (Ps. 9:16–17). There are those who object to this doctrine. But the same Christ that tells us of heaven and all of its glory also tells us of hell and its horrors. If that is not true, then we need to build a tomb over Christianity and say to the world, "There is no God. There is no good news. There is no such thing as salvation. There is no heaven, no hell, no hereafter."

If this doctrine is not true, then we have robbed the Bible of any excuse to be a valuable contribution to the lives of men. All we can do is to point to the Word of God and be reminded that the Word of God is our authority. It is the basis of what we believe. We cannot destroy portions of the Bible without destroying all of the Bible. The Bible claims to be completely the Word of God. Since that is true, we cannot take a pair of scissors and cut out of the Word of God something we do not like and throw it away. The doctrine of hell is a central teaching in the Word of God.

We must wrestle with the halting inconsistencies of the church's attitude. I must charge us with one of two great sins. The lesser sin is that of being tricked into not believing that there is a hell. The greater of the sins is that we have believed it with our minds but denied it with our actions. We live as if hell were not real. We approach evangelism as if it were an option for the church. If hell is a reality, if every man who dies goes either to heaven or hell, then this says something to us about what we are to do. We have been tricked into saying we believe it with our minds, but we deny it in our lives.

There is a double crime being committed against the souls of men today. It is first, a crime against men and women who, without Christ, are going to hell. But there is a greater crime in the lives of God's children. We have knowledge of the fact of eternal hell awaiting every man, yet we are silent about it. Our lives are a betrayal of Jesus Christ and his salvation. We do not care, and we do not care that we do not care! We are not interested. We have soothed ourselves and salved our consciences for so long. We have reveled in what we have done without realizing that we have been deceived and tricked into being quiet about the greatest news that the world has ever known.

The Certainty of Hell

Let us examine the certainty of hell. As far as we can be certain about anything, we can be certain that there is a hell. Hell is a logical necessity supported by three facts. First is the presence of law; second is the nature of man;

and third is the condition of the world.

There is an unwritten law in our world today. It is a real law. We suffer as a result of our violation of certain natural laws. There is a physical response to law. There is a moral response to law. The fact that man feels guilty is a response of his life to law. The fact that man feels discouragement and depression is evidence of the fact that there is a goal that he longs to achieve that he has not achieved. If mankind is immortal, as the Bible says and as we believe he is, then it certainly cannot wisely be assumed that this law will be cast aside when he dies. The presence of law indicates and necessitates this place called hell.

Man's nature also necessitates the fact of hell. Man is evil in his nature. He is not fit for fellowship with God. He is not a being that could be comfortable with God. That is why we do not have sinners crowding into church. That is why we have to go where they are. They do not want to come to church. That is the last place they want to be. They feel guilty, hostile, bitter, and resentful. That is the way people without Christ are. Man's nature is not right. It is not fit for fellowship with God. If the whole world went to heaven just as we are, soon heaven would be just like the earth is and would become hell.

World conditions necessitate a belief in some kind of punishment. How do we explain all the viciousness and brutality in the world today? How can we reconcile the irrationality, the absurdity, the insanity in the world today? What we see today are simply sparks from the lake which will burn with eternal godlessness. The facts of logic support this matter of the certainty of hell.

The character of God demands a hell. Contrary to what some people say, God is too good *not* to let people go to hell. What kind of God would he be to let people who had destroyed others, cursed and responded in wickedness all of their lifetimes, not receive the just punishment for the way they lived? He is a just God. In any system of justice there are two factors: reward and punishment. If we eliminate reward and punishment from any system of justice, we have destroyed justice. Justice is based upon the fact that someone needs to be rewarded and someone needs to be punished. If we eliminate that fact, we have eliminated justice altogether. It is an illogical expression of man's fantasy to eliminate punishment. God is too good not to punish. Hear what David said: "The Lord is known by the judgment which he executeth" (Ps. 9:16).

Logic supports the certainty of hell; the character of God demands it; and the Scripture confirms it. "A fire is kindled in mine anger, and shall burn unto the lowest hell, and shall consume the earth with her increase, and set on fire the foundations of the mountains" (Deut. 32:22). "The Son of man shall send forth his angels, and they shall gather out of his kingdom all things that offend, and them which do iniquity; And shall cast them into a furnace of fire: there shall be wailing and gnashing of teeth. Then shall the righteous shine forth as the sun in the kingdom of their Father. Who hath ears to hear, let him hear. So shall it be at the end of the world: the angels shall come forth, and sever the wicked from among the just, And shall cast them into the furnace of fire: there shall be wailing and gnashing of teeth. And these shall go away into everlasting punishment: but the righteous into life eternal" (Matt. 13:41–43,49–50; 25:46).

"If thy hand offend thee, cut it off: it is better for thee to enter into life maimed, than having two hands to go into hell, into the fire that never shall be quenched" (Mark 9:43). "The angels which kept not their first estate, but left their own habitation, he hath reserved in everlasting chains under darkness unto the judgment of the great day. Even as Sodom and Gomorrah, and the cities about them in like manner, giving themselves over to fornication, and going after strange flesh, are set forth for an example, suffering the vengeance of eternal fire" (Jude 6–7).

There are hundreds of Scriptures that tell us of the certainty of hell.

The Circumstances of Hell

What are the circumstances of hell? First of all, it is a literal place. There is today a place called hell, and when Jesus has returned there will also be a place called hell. If there is symbolism involved, there are two things that are true. One is that symbolism is only used to convey a truth that cannot be understood any other way. We use symbols in order to explain what something is like. Second, the symbol is always less severe than the real thing. Are we afraid of a picture of a fire? It will never burn us. It is a symbol of a fire. It just represents a fire, but we are not frightened by it.

However, we are afraid of a fire. The reality is far worse than the symbol. If God is using a symbol to help us understand something we could not understand otherwise, it is far worse than the symbol could ever be. The picture of hell given in the Bible conveys agony, panic, guilt, despair, loss, and so on. A thousand things are conveyed in the descriptions that are used. Whatever they represent is far worse.

The second thing the Bible tells us about the circumstances of hell is that it is eternal. This life is given to us to make some choices. God created man to have fellowship with him. He had angels who would come at his command, but they were not created with the choice of good and evil so that they could *choose* God. Satan was an angel who chose to rebel against God, but he could not repent. There is a difference in the nature of angels and the nature of man. Man can respond to God; and through repentance, man can be brought to God. God created us for that purpose. This life is for us to decide where we are to spend eternity. The wrath of God abides eternally. It is eternal fire. It is everlasting punishment. Read again the passages above, and bear in mind those adjectives that describe the length and nature of this state of hell.

The third thing about the circumstances of hell is that it is rational. Many believe that when we die, we cease to exist. It is appealing to believe that we can live as we please and, when we die, cease to exist. But the Bible tells us that hell is rational. Man in hell is conscious. He knows, he sees, he remembers, he grieves, he pleads, he thirsts, he hurts, he is exhausted, and he is forever dying but never dead. The nature of sin is still the same. Even in hell it continues to eat, gnaw, and destroy unendingly. In hell, there is the anguish of self-discovery. That is part of the rational aspect of it. It is worsened by memories of opportunities refused. The devil will have a heyday with folks down there reminding them of all the times they rejected Jesus. It is compounded by the fact that there is no hope. They will hear the gospel throughout eternity, but they cannot respond to it.

The Bible tells us also that the circumstances are unspeakably horrible. There is "weeping and gnashing of teeth." Have you ever had pain so severe you gritted your teeth to try to ease the pain? Have you ever hurt so bad that you screamed and cried out? God has fire and darkness that we do not know anything about. We just think we know what fire is. We just think we know what darkness is. Turn your imagination loose for a moment. Think of the most awful thing you could imagine. Think of despair. Think of when you lost a loved one or the tragedy of an accident. Think how your heart was shocked, how you were thrown into panic. Think how lonely you have felt when you were thousands of miles from home, when it seemed that no one knew or cared. Then multiply that a thousand times, and you have yet to describe the conditions of an eternal hell without God.

The frustration, the hopelessness, the anger, the madness, the suffering of our world is just a reminder to us of what hell is like. Stretch to infinity the absurdity and the senselessness of murder, the futility of prejudice, the ignorance and the idiocy of the way we destroy our lives, and the mad clawing at each other to get ahead, and we have hell.

The Crowds in Hell

Look with me at the crowds that will be in hell. Who will be there? "Know ye not that the unrighteous shall not inherit the kingdom of God? Be not deceived: neither fornicators, nor idolaters, nor adulterers, nor effeminate, nor abusers of themselves with mankind, Nor thieves, nor covetous, nor drunkards, nor revilers, nor extortioners, shall inherit the kingdom of God" (1 Cor. 6:9–10). Since they will not share the kingdom of God, they will be in hell.

"Whosoever was not found written in the book of life was cast into the lake of fire. But the fearful, and unbelieving, and the abominable, and murderers, and whoremongers, and sorcerers, and idolaters, and all liars, shall have their part in the lake which burneth with fire and birmstone: which is the second death" (Rev. 20:15; 21:8).

Who of us has not lied? lusted? been proud? We are all

listed here. Every man who has ever been born is listed. There is only one hope for us to be taken off that list, and that is for us to be forgiven. That is why forgiveness is so great. When we as liars are forgiven, in God's sight we have never lied. All unforgiven liars are going to hell. All forgiven immoral people are going to hell. When our immoral lives are brought to God, we are cleansed and forgiven and receive a new start. That is good news in a bad-news society. Forgiveness is total and complete. Unforgiveness is irrevocable.

The Contrast to Hell

Another chapter will discuss the contrast to hell in detail, but the view of hell is incomplete without this glorious contrast. "He carried me away in the spirit to a great and high mountain, and shewed me that great city. . . . And the city had no need of the sun, neither of the moon, to shine in it: for the glory of God did lighten it, and the Lamb is the light thereof. And the nations of them which are saved shall walk in the light of it: and the kings of the earth do bring their glory and honour into it. And the gates of it shall not be shut at all by day: for there shall be no night there. And they shall bring the glory and honour of the nations into it. And there shall in no wise enter into it any thing that defileth, neither whatsoever worketh abomination, or maketh a lie: but they which are written in the Lamb's book of life. And he shewed me a pure river of water of life, clear as crystal, proceeding out of the throne of God and of the Lamb. And there shall be no more curse: but the throne of God and of the Lamb shall be in it; and his servants shall serve him: And they shall see his face; and his name shall be in their foreheads. And there shall be no night there; and they need no candle, neither light of the sun; for the

Lord God giveth them light: and they shall reign for ever
and ever" (Rev. 21:10,23–27; 22:1,3–5).

The contrast is caused by Christ! There is sin in the world
and there is a hell awaiting; but there is a fountain filled
with blood, and sinners plunged beneath that flood lose all
their guilty stains. Heaven is given in great contrast to hell.
It is a city of light, love, happiness, and joy. There is no
curse; there is no sin. There are no pains, guilts, tears, or
miseries. The former things have passed away. There is no
night. We live in the full blaze of one eternal day. Our home
will be everlasting. Our glory will be eternal. Our crown
will be never fading. Our lives will be immortal. Pleasures,
riches, honors eternal are ours. So we turn our eyes above,
convinced and convicted of the reality of hell.

The most vivid description of hell we could imagine is
on Calvary. Come with me outside the walls of the city. It
is a blistering, hot day in an arid, desert, dusty climate. It
is so hot that one's pores cry for refreshment. Suddenly in
the blistering heat of noonday, the blackness of midnight
shrouds around the earth. We are surrounded by this darkness as we stand before a cross upon which Jesus Christ
hangs dying. If our eyes could see in the darkness, we would
see the blood curdling upon his face. We would hear the
groans issuing from his swollen lips. We would see the physical suffering coupled with the spiritual anguish. There on
that cross Jesus Christ extinguished the flames of hell for
every sinner who would repent.

God made us for himself. But we are not fit to be with
him. By our sin we have alienated ourselves from God. But
we do not have to go to hell. We can accept God's way of
salvation through Jesus Christ. We who have been saved
have been left in this world to be a part of heralding the
truth of salvation from hell. When we hold the reality of

hell up against our lack of dedication, we can understand something of the heartache of God. He saw his son die an agonizing death. His death was a picture, a mirror of hell. He entrusted to his disciples the message of salvation that was purchased and perfected by that Son's death and subsequent resurrection. Hell is a reality, and our task is to trumpet the good news of God's perfect provision through Jesus Christ.

12
The Disease of Sin

An understanding of the doctrine of sin is vital to understanding our relationship with God. Sin is anything that is contrary to the law and will of God. The basic attitude of sin makes God irrelevant to life. Sin makes self to be God and reduces God to the level of humanity.

Sin is an act. It is to violate or to disregard the will or the purposes of God. Sin is a state. It is a state of unrighteousness, of evil in our hearts and lives. Sin is a nature. It is a nature that is at enmity, at odds with God. Sin is a lie. It started out as a lie, and it continues to be the epitome of falsehood. Sin is a delusion. It is not what it seems to be. It promises big. It produces zero. Sin is darkness. It shrouds the life and the heart with the blackness of a thousand midnights. Sin is separation from all that is good, meaningful and fulfilling. Sin is perversion. In its essence, sin is the perversion of good. When something is used for a purpose that was not intended, it is thus perverted and abused.

Sin is servitude, for one who sins finds himself enslaved by sin. Sin is emptiness. Sin is a mistake. Whenever one enters into sin, he is always the epitome of foolishness. Sin corrupts the soul. It defiles everything about. It cheapens, debases, and defaces all that it touches.

Those who keep on sinning are against God, for every sin is done against the will of God. And you know that he became a man so that he could take away our sins, and that there is no sin in him, no missing of God's will at any time in any way. So if we stay close to him, obedient to him, we won't be sinning either; but as for those who keep on sinning, they should realize this: They sin because they have never really known him or become his. Oh, dear children, don't let anyone deceive you about this: if you are constantly doing what is good, it is because you are good, even as he is. But if you keep on sinning, it shows that you belong to Satan, who since he first began to sin has kept steadily at it. But the Son of God came to destroy these works of the devil. The person who has been born into God's family does not make a practice of sinning, because now God's life is in him; so he can't keep on sinning, for this new life has been born into him and controls him—he has been born again" (1 John 3:4–9, TBL).

John 3 contains a tremendous emphasis on sin and deals with our love for each other. We can readily see that whenever there is a lack of love, a lack of compassion, a lack of concern for each other, the cause is always sin in active operation in the lives of God's children.

The Root of Sin

Sin originated with Satan. When Paul spoke about ordaining a bishop or a pastor, he said that he must "not [be] a novice [not someone that is immature], lest being lifted up with pride he fall into the condemnation of the devil" (1 Tim. 3:6). The sin of Satan was pride. Concerning the origin of Satan, God's Word very vividly declares, "Thou wast perfect in thy ways from the day that thou wast created, till iniquity was found in thee" (Ezek. 28:15). "How you are fallen from heaven, O Lucifer, son of the morning! How you are cut down to the ground—mighty though you were against the nations of the world. For you said to yourself,

'I will ascend to heaven and rule the angels. I will take
the highest throne. I will preside on the Mount of Assembly
far away in the north. I will climb to the highest heavens
and be like the Most High.' But instead, you will be brought
down to the pit of hell, down to its lowest depths" (Isa.
14:12–15, TLB).

Sin started in Satan's experience. Satan was the highest,
most beautiful creation of God. He is described in superla-
tives (Ezek. 28). Throughout the Word of God we have the
report that Lucifer was the brightest of the angels. We do
not know why Satan sinned. We can speculate, but it is much
better for us to accept the fact that it did not please God
to tell us how or why sin got into Satan's life. God simply
tells us that it did. "Thou wast perfect . . . til iniquity was
found in thee" (Ezek. 28:15). The iniquity that was found
in Lucifer was the sin of pride (Isa. 14). He had a deep
ambition to be God. That is the very essence of sin. This
was the sin of Satan and continues to be the root of all sin.

It is easy to see why the New Testament places such a
great condemnation upon pride. Sin is to lift self up to pride
and prefer what we think to what God declares. Sin originated with Satan, but it continues in man's sinful nature.
It continues in the choices we make. We are not guilty as
sinners because of Satan's sin, but because of our own sin.
The Bible makes that very clear. There is a difference between original sin and actual sin. Original sin is that inherited
tendency which every man has to rebel against God. We
are condemned to hell because of actual sin. Our choices
are asserted, and we choose to sin.

The Reality of Sin

How does sin express itself? What form does it take? First
of all, sin is described in the words of John as "the transgression of the law." The word transgress means to go across.

God has set a standard. Man transgresses as he goes across God's law and purposes. He violates, he defies, he rebels against God's laws. No one ever breaks God's laws. We may defy them, but we do not break them. We are broken by them. If I jump off the top of a building, I am not breaking the law of gravity; I am breaking my neck! I may defy the law of gravity, but I do not break it. I am broken by it. It is this way with all of God's laws. God's physical laws are absolute. We abide by the physical laws of God. That is why we can put a man on the moon. That is why we can predict the weather. That is why we know that summer comes after spring and autumn after summer. We know the cycle because the laws of God are absolute.

God is just as rigid about his spiritual and moral laws. Sin is to defy, to transgress the law of God. His laws are given to protect us, help us, and guide us. They are for our encouragement and benefit. We only hurt ourselves when we defy the laws of God. God is just as rigid in the enforcement of his spiritual and moral laws as he is his physical laws. If one commits immorality and thus defiles the body God has given to him, he can be sure his sins will find him out. Whatever we sow, that we will reap.

Sin is rebellion and revolt against God. It is to assert a spirit of false independence. Notice the word *false* because we are never really independent. We like to think we are. If we are not controlled by God, we will be controlled by something else. It is a false spirit of independence that says, "I am going to be independent of God." We will be dependent upon something else that will be more tragic than we can possibly imagine.

Further, the Bible tells us that sin is expressed in the omission of good. "To him that knoweth to do good, and doeth it not, to him it is sin" (James 4:17). We can sin by doing

nothing. Suppose your mother lived with you, and she became unable to care for herself. You place her in a bed in
a bedroom, but you never feed her, never take any water
or nourishment to her. You do not help her in any way,
and she dies. Why did she die? She died at your hands just
as surely as if you had taken a pistol, put it to her head,
and pulled the trigger. You killed her, not by what you did,
but by what you did not do.

The absence of evil does not make a righteous person.
The absence of viciousness and unkindness does not make
a good person. Sin is the omission of good. If we know to
do good and do not do it, it is sin. The absence of obedience
to the will of God at any point in our lives is sin.

Unbelief toward God is sin. "Whatsoever is not of faith
is sin" (Rom. 14:23). Whenever we let unbelief assert itself
in our lives, that is sin. We use mild words to describe unbelief. We excuse things as being a shame or a tragedy. God
calls it sin. Sin is unbelief. "Without faith it is impossible
to please him; for he that cometh to God must believe that
he is, and that he is a rewarder of them that diligently seek
him" (Heb. 11:6). To be without faith is to have unbelief.
Whatever is not of faith is sin. Sin expresses itself in lack
of faith, in unbelief.

We are sinners by nature. We inherit the tendency to
sin. Every child, wherever he is born, when he reaches an
age where he can understand between right and wrong,
will choose wrong. Sin expresses itself in all our lives. Satan
tries to influence us, but he does not force us or compel
us. We make our own choices. All of us are sinners by nature
and by choice.

The Bible says much about sin in its universality. " 'No
one is good—no one in all the world is innocent.' No one
has ever really followed God's paths, or even truly wanted

to. Every one has turned away; all have gone wrong. No
one anywhere has kept on doing what is right; not one.
Their talk is foul and filthy like the stench from an open
grave. Their tongues are loaded with lies. Everything they
say has in it the sting and poison of deadly snakes. Their
mouths are full of cursing and bitterness. They are quick
to kill, hating anyone who disagrees with them. Wherever
they go they leave misery and trouble behind them, and
they have never known what it is to feel secure or enjoy
God's blessing. They care nothing about God nor what he
thinks of them. So the judgment of God lies very heavily
upon the Jews, for they are responsible to keep God's laws
instead of doing all these evil things; not one of them has
any excuse; in fact, all the world stands hushed and guilty
before Almighty God. Now do you see it? No one can ever
be made right in God's sight by doing what the law commands. For the more we know of God's laws, the clearer
it becomes that we aren't obeying them; his laws serve only
to make us see that we are sinners. But now God has shown
us a different way to heaven—not by 'being good enough'
and trying to keep his laws, but by a new way (though not
new, really, for the Scriptures told about it long ago). Now
God says he will accept and acquit us—declare us 'not
guilty'—if we trust Jesus Christ to take away our sins. And
we all can be saved in this same way, by coming to Christ,
no matter who we are or what we have been like. Yes, all
have sinned; all fall short of God's glorious ideal" (Rom. 3:10–
23,TLB).

"When Adam sinned, sin entered the entire human race.
His sin spread death throughout all the world, so everything
began to grow old and die, for all sinned" (Rom. 5:12,TLB).
The reality of sin expresses itself in all of our lives.

The Realm of Sin

Sin originates and operates in the human heart. Sin is conceived in the heart. It is in the heart that lust is harbored. It is in the heart that we commit ourselves to rebellion and revolt against God. Sin operates first in the human heart; then it operates in human action. Our actions are simply the results of what is in our hearts. If we are concerned about sins, we will categorize them as being bad and not so bad and begin to think that sins in themselves have a nature or a degree of evil. That is not true. There is sin in the human heart, and that causes evil action.

We need to be concerned about sin. Sin is in the heart, and there has to be a deep confession for our attitude of rebellion and revolt against God. If all we do is confess specific sins to God and never get around to repenting of the sin in our hearts, we will always be hounded, haunted, and dominated by sin. People who have particularly harmful habits, such as narcotics, smoking, drinking, gossiping, and so on, must do more than simply confess those sins. Sin is that attitude of rebellion, resentment, and hostility toward God that is in our hearts, and we must deal with that.

The Results of Sin

There are three results of sin. The first is physical death. "And as it is appointed unto men once to die, but after this the judgment" (Heb. 9:27). "No man can live forever. All will die. Who can rescue his life from the power of the grave?" (Ps. 89:48,TLB). Physical death is the first result of sin. We spend a great deal of time being concerned about and worrying about physical death. But physical death is a blessing. Because of man's choice to rebel against God and to sin against God, if God had not passed the sentence of physical death, then the earth would soon become hell itself. Man would have endless time to get bad. Death is a blessing because every generation gets a fresh start. If man had never died, imagine how wicked the earth would have become since the Garden of Eden.

By the time of Noah, which was just a few hundred years, "the wickedness of man was great in the earth, and that every imagination of the thoughts of his heart was only evil continually" (Gen. 6:5). Man was 100 percent flesh. He was like a beast, a wild animal. That may be why God reduced the life expectancy to around seventy years of age. Back then, it was not unusual of someone to live five hundred or even nine hundred years. But physical death came. We need to realize that had God not passed the sentence of physical death as a result of sin, this world would have been destroyed a long time before now. This world would have been a tragic place for anyone to try to live. As it is, every baby born has a fresh chance to build his own life and to choose God's way. Physical death is the first result of sin.

Secondly, spiritual death is a result of sin. "And you hath he quickened, who were dead in trespasses and sins" (Eph. 2:1). The Bible describes those separated from God as being dead. Jesus said "The hour is coming, and now is, when the dead shall hear the voice of the Son of God: and they that hear shall live" (John 5:25). He was not talking about corpses in graveyards. He was talking about the living dead, those who were spiritually dead.

To be spiritually dead means two things. First, our minds are affected. The spiritually dead cannot understand the Scripture because they are not spiritually discerning (1 Cor. 2:14). Their minds have been clouded and veiled. Sin is irrational. Do not try to explain it. Have you ever done something and wondered why you did it? The reason is that sin is unreasonable—it is irrational.

Spiritual death affects the will. Jesus said, "Verily, verily, I say unto you, Whosoever committeth sin is the servant of sin" (John 8:34). His will is bound. He will always make the wrong choice.

Spiritual death affects the conscience. There is an old saying, "Let your conscience be your guide." That is the worse thing we can do. We can teach our consciences to do anything. People who are spiritually dead have their consciences "seared" (1 Tim. 4:2) and calloused. They begin to call black white and white black, and soon they cannot tell the difference. We can take any sin and sear our conscience to it.

There is a third result of sin. It is eternal death. When on dies spiritually, if he is not born twice, he will die twice. He will die physically, and he will die eternally. The second death is the payment for sin that is not atoned for by the second birth. "The Son of man shall send forth his angels, and they shall gather out of his kingdom all things that offend, and them which do iniquity; And shall cast them into a furnace of fire: there shall be wailing and gnashing of teeth" (Matt. 13:41–42). "These shall go away into everlasting punishment: but the righteous into life eternal" (Matt. 25:46). The result of sin is eternal death.

The Remedy for Sin

Everyone can give living testimony to the biblical truth about sin. But praise God! The Bible declares the remedy for sin. That is why Jesus Christ came into the world. He came to be the remedy for sin. As God's remedy for sin, Jesus Christ saves us from the guilt of sin. When we confess our sins to God, we are no longer guilty under God. "There is therefore now no condemnation to them which are in

Christ Jesus, who walk not after the flesh, but after the Spirit" (Rom. 8:1).

"If we walk in the light, as he is in the light, we have fellowship one with another, and the blood of Jesus Christ his son cleanseth us from all sin. If we confess our sins, he is faithful and just to forgive us our sins, and to cleanse us from all unrighteousness. And he is the propitiation for our sins: and not for ours only, but also for the sins of the whole world" (1 John 1:7,9; 2:2).

When we come to Jesus Christ, we are saved from the guilt of sin. We are forgiven, and it is just as though it had never happened. We can start over again. We do not have to live on the basis of our sin. Not one of us wants that guilt to be held over us like a sword of Damocles. We do not have to live that way. The gospel declares that we can be free, for "ye shall know the truth, and the truth shall make you free. If the son . . . shall make you free, ye shall be free indeed" (John 8:32,36). Not guilty! That is the salvation which Jesus Christ offers to us, salvation from the guilt of sin.

But salvation also comes from the power of sin. "Greater is he that is in you, than he that is in the world" (1 John 4:4). The apostle Paul said, "There hath no temptation taken you but such as is common to man: but God is faithful, who will not suffer you to be tempted above that ye are able; but will with the temptation also make a way to escape, that ye may be able to bear it" (1 Cor. 10:13). Jesus Christ saves us from the guilt of sin and then delivers us from the power of sin. We do not have to be bound by our sin. There is freedom from the power of sin.

If we are still under the power of sin, it is because we have been disobedient. There has to be a spiritual discipline to lives. Everyone wants to do better. But just desiring it does not make it happen. We must have a discipline to spiritual truth in our lives. If we want to learn how to do something, we have to learn slowly and practice.

When I learned to type, I did not start typing eighty words a minute. I had to learn the keyboard. I had to practice diligently. Finally, after many long hours of discipline, I developed a skill. The spiritual life is no different. The fact that we are saved does not mean that we are instantaneously holy and mature.

One tragic thing that has happened to Christianity is the fact that we will hear about someone's being saved and immediately have him up preaching somewhere. What does he know? He does not know what has happened to him. He cannot even explain it. Yet all of a sudden, he is seen as an authority. There is no such thing as instantaneous spiritual maturity. We are living in the day of instant everything, but not instant spirituality. It takes time and discipline for God to fully deliver us from the power of sin. If we are expecting God to do it in one great "zap," forget it. It will never happen. He delivers from the power of sin, but his work has to be coupled with our dedication, determination and discipline. The power of sin is real, but Jesus Christ delivers us from that power as we continue in a diligent, dedicated, disciplined life.

He also delivers us from the penalty of sin. When we are saved, we will not go to hell. That judgment of God upon our sin is transferred to Jesus Christ. He died for us. He bore our agony. "For he hath made him to be sin for us . . . that we might be made the righteousness of God in him" (2 Cor. 5:21). Everything that he could not tolerate, he became for us. When we are saved, we are saved from the penalty of sin.

13
The Necessity of Repentance

Repentance is one of the most crucial themes of the Word of God. If we do not understand what the Bible says about repentance, we will not understand what salvation really is. Man has to repent before he can be saved. The words for repentance in the Old Testament are used more than six-hundred times. In the New Testament there are three basic words translated repentance. These words are used in excess of one hundred times.

When we study the history of the early church, we find that repentance was the central theme, the cutting edge of its message. John the Baptist came preaching: "Repent ye, for the kingdom of heaven is at hand" (Matt. 3:2).

When Jesus Christ had emerged from the wilderness, victor over temptation and over Satan, he began to preach: "Repent: for the kingdom of heaven is at hand" (Matt. 4:17). When Jesus commissioned the twelve to preach, "They went out, and preached that men should repent" (Mark 6:12).

Luke declared, "And that repentance and remission of sins should be preached in his name among all nations, beginning at Jerusalem" (24:47).

When Peter and John gave restoration to the lame man at the Gate Beautiful, his healing caused a great stir among the people. They all gathered on Solomon's porch to hear Peter. The message Simon Peter delivered was, "Repent ye therefore, and be converted, that your sins may be blotted out, when the times of refreshing shall come from the presence of the Lord" (Acts 3:19).

When the disciples were arrested and brought back to give a reason why they were continuing to preach, they simply said, "We ought to obey God rather than men. The God of our fathers raised up Jesus, whom ye slew and hanged on a tree. Him hath God exalted with his right hand to be a Prince and a Saviour, for to give repentance to Israel, and forgiveness of sins" (Acts 5:29–31).

When Paul stood among the philosophers on Mars Hill, he said to them, "In him [Jesus Christ] we live, and move, and have our being. . . . And the times of this ignorance God winked at; but now commandeth all men everywhere to repent" (Acts 17:28,30). When Paul stood before King Agrippa giving his defense, he turned to the king and declared that God had given him a message that men "should repent and turn to God, and do works meet for repentance" (Acts 26:20).

When Jesus Christ sent a message to his churches as recorded by the apostle John, he said, "Remember therefore from whence thou art fallen, and repent, and do the first works; or else I will come unto thee quickly. . . . Remember therefore how thou hast received and heard, and hold fast, and repent. . . . Be zealous therefore, and repent" (Rev. 2:5; 3:3,19).

One thing is clear: Sinners must repent. God's mercy and God's grace to sinful humanity is based upon man's repentance. His grace is given in response to the repentance of the hearts of men.

It is clear that saints need to repent. We do not stop repenting when we are saved. In fact, when we are saved, we do not have a full understanding of what repentance is. It is a continuing experience rather than an act terminating at a point in time. It is a growing and enlarging experience for the Christian. I repented when I first believed, and I have repented continually ever since. Repentance is simply recognizing our need for grace. Without repentance, we would not have an awareness that we need grace. Grace cannot operate where repentance has not opened the door.

The Reason for Repentance

The question was asked of Jesus, "What about the Galileans, whose blood Pilate had mingled with their sacrifices?" They were martyrs. They were suggesting to Jesus that the Galileans were a special people who should have a special reward for the way Pilate treated them. "And Jesus answering said unto them, Suppose ye that these Galileans were sinners above all the other Galileans, because they suffered such things? I tell you, Nay: but, except ye repent, ye shall all likewise perish" (Luke 13:2–3).

Jesus in effect said, "Regardless of what you may have encountered, regardless of what you have done, regardless of how good you think your response to the experiences of life have been, there is a necessity for you to repent or perish."

We only have one inevitable choice—repent or perish. That is the choice of mankind. Sin is destructive. Sin will destroy everything that is good, noble, and holy in our lives. When we violate God's law and sin, we incur the penalty of sin, which is always death and destruction. Sin decays, debases, and defaces everything it touches. The first and unavoidable step toward deliverance from sin is repentance.

If we do not repent, there is no victory over sin, no freedom from sin and guilt. Sin will haunt us and hound us and never leave us alone unless we repent. We have an inevitable alternative. We must either repent or perish. That is why the Bible is so strong at the point of repentance.

The whole point of the story of Lazarus and the rich man (Luke 16) is that if we do not repent of our sins in this life, we will be separated from God in the life to come. The rich man spurned God's grace and God's love. He spurned repentance and delighted in sin and rebellion. In this life he fared sumptuously; but in hell and in torment, he is separated from the goodness of God for eternity. That is our alternative. No man can be saved without repentance.

One of the great tragedies today is that there is such an easy attitude toward conversion. Repentance is the most serious business in the world. It is the response of a broken heart over sin. Without it no man can be saved. Being saved is not a matter of loving God. Being saved is a matter of turning from our sinfulness to God. Without repentance there is no salvation.

The Nature of Repentance

What is repentance? First of all, notice what it is not. Repentance is not regret. If we have ever done something foolish, we regret that we did it. But regret is not repentance. Regret may lead us to repentance, but regret by itself is not repentance.

Repentance is not conviction. "The devils also believe, and tremble" (James 2:19). They are convicted of their rebellion, and they believe the right things, but they are still lost because conviction by itself is not enough. It may lead us to repentance, but conviction is not repentance.

Repentance is not remorse. The Bible says that Judas "repented himself" and then went out and hanged himself (Matt. 27:3–5). The word translated "repent" in that passage is a word which refers to remorse. He was eaten up with guilt and remorse. He hated himself for what he had done, but that is not repentance. Nor is it penitence or sorrow. Most of us are sorry when we get caught, but that is not repentance.

Reformation is not repentance. Many times we do something and try to make amends for it. We determine to clean up our lives and change our ways. That is not repentance.

Repentance is not confession. We may confess what our sin is, but confession is not repentance. The best illustration is the prodigal son. When he came to himself, he confessed, "I have sinned." Then he said, "I will arise and go to my father" (Luke 15:18). Repentance came when he arose and came home. Repentance is not confession.

On the positive side, repentance is an about-face. When we repent, our lives are transformed. When we repent, God works a miracle in our lives. God comes into our lives and changes us. Repentance means that we are going one way and then do an about-face; we change directions. Repentance lays hold to the power of God that changes and transforms everything that we are.

Secondly, repentance is a change of mind and heart. The idea is that of a complete reorientation of thoughts. We do not think the same way as before. There is a new way of looking at life, a complete reversal. "Sow to yourselves in righteousness, reap in mercy; break up your fallow ground" (Hos. 10:12). Fallow ground is that which is uncultivated— virgin land that has not been tilled or sown. Repentance gets down into the very depths of our being, breaking up the fallow ground. A change takes place. That which has been unproductive becomes productive.

That results in a change of judgment. In Acts 26 Paul talked about the things he did to the saints. He put them in prison and put them to death. He mocked them and cursed them when they died. But after God came into his life, a change of judgment came into his life. Before he was saved, he judged them guilty and worthy of death. After his conversion, he judged them as the saints of god. He had a change of judgment. When we have repented, our judgment changes. The things we once hated, we now love. The things we once loved, we now hate.

Repentance brings about a reversal of feeling. The best example of this is Job. Job maintained that he was a just man, a righteous man—but in chapter 42 he said, "I abhor myself, and repent in dust and ashes" (v. 6). He had a change of attitude toward himself. He had thought he was a good person; but when he saw God, his soul repented of his sinfulness. Repentance is a reversal of feeling.

It is a change of attitudes and actions. Paul speaks about the change in the lives of the believers in Thessalonica (1 Thess. 1:9–10). Repentance produced that change.

Repentance results in a transformation of affections. "Through thy precepts I get understanding: therefore I hate every false way" (Ps. 119:104). We love the things that are lovely and hate the things that are evil.

If repentance means anything at all, it means a deep mourning for our sins. When Isaiah saw God high and lifted up, he said, "Woe is me! for I am undone; because I am a man of unclean lips, and I dwell in the midst of a people of unclean lips" (Isa. 6:5). After David was confronted with his sin by Nathan the prophet, he fell upon his face and cried before God. "The sacrifices of God are a broken spirit: a broken and a contrite heart, O God, thou wilt not despise" (Ps. 51:17). It is distressing to see people make decisions that seem to be taken so lightly. There is only one proper way to come to God, and that is with a broken heart. Repentance is a deep mourning for having committed sin.

The most common word used for *repent* in the Old Testament is translated to sigh, to groan, to lament. There must be a deep sadness and a sorrow for sin that causes us to cast ourselves upon the mercy of God. That is the essence of repentance.

The other word in the Old Testament means to turn, to turn away, or to return. If we have not turned away from sin and returned unto God, we have not repented. If sin is seen only as an affront to friends or society, then we will not be burdened about it. When David sinned he killed Uriah; he committed immorality with Bathsheba; he sinned against the people because he was their political and spiritual leader. But when he came to confess his sin, he said, "Against thee, and thee only, have I sinned, and done this evil" (Ps. 51:4). He had sinned against Uriah. He had sinned against Bathsheba. He had sinned against the people. But his sin was basically against God. David could have stayed comfortable with the fact that he had done something wrong against his fellowmen. But when he realized that his sin was against God, the knowledge broke his heart.

Engage in a little test with me for a moment. Think of the people you love the most—the person who is the sweetest, most gracious person in the world to you. Think of someone whose life you cherish the most, the person who is most like Jesus to you, the person who is always responding in love and grace to you. Now, pretend that that person is seated by you. As you turn, you spit in his face. You take your fist and pound him in the face. You hit him again and again and again, until his face is virtually destroyed. Then you curse him with all the bitterness of vicious hatred. Then with a mocking laugh, you laugh at him.

You say, "I can't do that." But we have done that and more to God! Every time we sin, we have done that to God.

He loves us so much he sent his Son to die for us; yet our response to him has been to hate him, to curse him, to spit upon him, to beat him by our sin. We have not repented until we recognize that our sin is against him. There is no union with God apart from that kind of repentance. Repentance involves a spiritual divorce. When we repent, we turn from our sin forever. That is the essence of repentance.

Repentance is always accompanied by faith—"testifying both to the Jews, and also to the Greeks, repentance toward God, and faith toward our Lord Jesus Christ" (Acts 20:21). Repentance and faith are part and parcel of the same thing. No one truly believes in Christ who does not repent. We cannot really believe in Christ without repenting. The man who believes repents. The repentant soul puts his trust in God. No one believes the gospel and rests in it for salvation until he judges himself a sinner before God and turns in repentance to him.

14
Blood Atonement

Blood atonement is something we do not like to talk about. To us blood is a terrible thing. We are all frightened by it. Imagine how Adam and Eve felt when they saw blood. God had created Adam and Eve, and they sinned. When God began to deal with their sin, he killed an animal in order to give covering for their nakedness. Their nakedness was symbolic of their guilt. They did not know they were naked until they sinned. Then their consciences were livened, and they were aware that they had rebelled against God.

So God used the blood of an animal to cover their shame. Adam and Eve saw the innocent animal writhing and shuddering in pain and agony, bleeding to death. It was a terrible thing to them. We too recoil at the sight of blood. Everything that the sight of blood did to Adam and Eve and everything it does to us, however, is as nothing compared to what our sins do to the heart of the Holy God.

"Just think how much more surely the blood of Christ will transform our lives and hearts. His sacrifice frees us from the worry of having to obey the old rules, and makes us want to serve the living God. For by the help of the eternal Holy Spirit, Christ willingly gave himself to God to die for our sins—he being perfect, without a single sin or fault. Christ came with this new agreement so that all who are invited may come and have forever all the wonders God has promised them. For Christ died to rescue them from the penalty of the sins they had committed while still under that old system. In fact we can say that under the old agreement almost everything was cleansed by sprinkling it with blood, and without the shedding of blood there is no forgiveness of sins" (Heb. 9:14–15,22, TLB).

There are two reasons why people object to this doctrine of the blood atonement. One is that they have an inadequate view of sin. Many think that sin is an insignificant thing. Unfortunately, sin is not on the surface. It is something that is in the heart. It is an attitude of rebellion and resistance against God. That attitude is the world's greatest tragedy because it separates and alienates us from God. More than that, it is an assault on a Holy God who has never done anything but love us. We need to grasp the real meaning of what sin is.

The second reason people object to the doctrine of the blood atonement is that they have an inadequate view of God. Many do not understand the holiness of God. It is difficult to imagine a God who is so holy that he cannot look upon sin. We become calloused and accustomed to our surroundings. God can never get accustomed to sin. God can never tolerate sin. Those who object to the blood atonement simply do not understand the doctrine of a holy God.

Christ's death is mentioned 175 times in the New Testament. The New Testament tells us Jesus Christ came to die: "Since we, God's children, are human beings—made of flesh and blood—he became flesh and blood too by being born in human form; for only as a human being could he die and in dying break the power of the devil who had the power of death" (Heb. 2:14, TLB). He was born to die. He came into the world to go to the cross. In the narrative of the Gospels stands the shadow of the cross. We cannot separate salvation from the blood of Jesus.

A Unique Salvation

This blood atonement is a unique salvation. "Without the shedding of blood there is no forgiveness of sins" (Heb. 9:22, TLB). When we speak of salvation, we are not talking about *a* way in which a man may be saved. We are talking about *the only way* a man may be saved—salvation purchased by the death of Jesus Christ. "There is none other name under heaven given among men, whereby we must be saved" (Acts 4:12). It is through Jesus Christ and his atoning sacrifice for us that men are saved.

This unique salvation has several descriptions in the New Testament. It is called a "ransom" (Matt. 20:28). A ransom is paid so that someone who is held captive may be free. When Jesus Christ shed his blood, he paid the ransom for our sins so that we might be released from the bondage of sin and be free. We are bound by sin until we are set free by Jesus Christ. His blood atonement for us is a ransom in our behalf.

Jesus' sacrifice is also called a "propitiation." The word itself means a favorable report. The idea is that man's sin has rendered an unfavorable report to God. Our sin has alienated us from God. When Jesus died, his death propitiated God's holiness—gave a favorable report to God's holiness about us. When we are saved, we are cleansed from our sins. Although we once stood condemned, now we are accepted. Although we were alienated from the presence of God, we are now joined to the family of God. He is the propitiation for God's holiness.

"Herein is love, not that we loved God, but that he loved

us, and sent his Son to be the propitiation for our sins" (1 John 4:10). "And he is the propitiation for our sins: and not for ours only, but also for the sins of the whole world" (1 John 2:2). That means that the death of Jesus Christ is the basis upon which a loving God deals in mercy with the world. He propitiates God's holiness and unites us with the Father. Nothing else does that. This is a unique salvation.

If we apply *saved* or *salvation* in any of the contexts we find in the world, each of them is incomplete. They are all temporary. "I narrowly escaped an accident, but I was saved." However, I am going to die anyway. My salvation at the point of being spared is a very temporary and incomplete thing. In whatever context we use it, the idea of salvation is incomplete. But this unique salvation is complete. "Wherefore He is able to save them to the uttermost that come unto God by him" (Heb. 7:25). *Uttermost* is a superlative. It speaks of perfection and completeness.

A Costly Salvation

Secondly, salvation is costly. "He is the mediator of the new Testament, that by means of death . . ." (Heb. 9;15). We take forgiveness so easily. It is as though we say, "Please forgive me"; God says, "I forgive you"; and we say, "OK, thanks" and go our way. But salvation cost Jesus Christ everything.

It cost him his holiness. The perfect, holy Son of God gave up his holiness in order to bring salvation to me. He became sin for us (2 Cor. 5:21). He did not commit a sin, but he literally became sin.

He gave up his glory in heaven. He who was God himself left heaven to come here and to bring us salvation. Salvation is not something to be taken for granted. "Christ also hath once suffered for sins . . . being put to death in the flesh,

but quickened by the Spirit" (1 Peter 3:18). "Christ our passover is sacrificed for us" (1 Cor. 5:6). "Surely he hath borne
our griefs, and carried our sorrows: yet we did esteem him
stricken, smitten of God, and afflicted. But he was wounded
for our transgressions, he was bruised for our iniquities: the
chastisement of our peace was upon him; and with his stripes
we are healed" (Isa. 53:4–5). This blood-bought salvation is
a costly thing. If we would dwell upon the cost of our salvation it would make a difference in our lives.

An Available Salvation

This blood-bought salvation is an available salvation. It
does not do much good to hear of a salvation that is not
available. If it is not available, it holds no attraction to us.
The wonderful thing about the blood atonement is that it
is available to us. "For God so loved the world, that he gave
his only begotten Son, that whosoever believeth in him
should not perish, but have everlasting life" (John 3:16). It
is available for all people. "This is good and acceptable in
the sight of God our Saviour; Who will have all men to be
saved, and to come unto the knowledge of the truth. For
there is one God, and one mediator between God and men,
the man Christ Jesus; Who gave himself a ransom for *all*"
(1 Tim. 2:3–6). "Therefore we both labour and suffer re-
proach, because we trust in the living God, who is the Saviour
of all men, specially of those that believe" (1 Tim. 4:10).

It is available through the grace and mercy of God. "By
grace are ye saved through faith; and that not of yourselves:
it is the gift of God: Not of works, lest any should boast"
(Eph. 2:8–9). It is an available salvation to every person who
will receive it.

There are simple conditions for us to meet. "As many as
received him, to them gave he power to become the sons

of God" (John 1:12). We just receive it. The only way we can get a gift is to receive it. "The wages of sin is death; but the gift of God is eternal life through Jesus Christ our Lord" (Rom. 6:23). Paul said, "Testifying both to the Jews, and also to the Greeks, repentance toward God, and faith toward our Lord Jesus Christ" (Acts 20:21). We receive this salvation by repenting and trusting. If we do not truly repent, we do not truly believe. If we do not truly believe, we do not truly repent. One without the other is incomplete.

A Purposeful Salvation

It is a purposeful salvation. God saved us for a reason. He did not save us to go to heaven, or we would already be there. He saved us for a present purpose. We are his workmanship, created in Christ Jesus unto good works, which God hath before ordained that we should walk in them" (Eph. 2:10). When we were saved, God intended for us to express in our lives what he had done through us.

The apostle Paul often referred to our maintaining good works and our diligence in producing a godly life. He referred often to the fact that we have a responsibility to the world in which we live. This is God's way of reminding us that we have a purposeful salvation. It is sad when a Christian does not know why he was saved. Anyone who does not have a deep awareness of the purpose of his salvation will always be unhappy in his faith and inconsistent in his Christian life.

An Eternal Salvation

This blood atonement is not temporary. It is final, permanent. Hebrews 9:15 speaks of an "eternal inheritance." Jesus is called "the author of eternal salvation unto all them that obey him" (Heb. 5:9). By his own blood he entered in once into the holy place, having obtained eternal redemption for us" (Heb. 9:12). Since salvation is eternal, it will never end. "My sheep hear my voice, and I know them, and they follow me: And I give unto them eternal life; and they shall never perish, neither shall any man pluck them out of my hand" (John 10:27–28). If one man ever gave his heart to Jesus and received salvation and lost his salvation, then Jesus is a liar. Jesus declared, "they shall never perish." That is the consistent message of the Word of God.

Let us examine the first passover in Egypt. God said, "I will pass through the land of Egypt this night, and will smite all the firstborn in the land of Egypt, both man and beast; and against all the gods of Egypt I will execute judgment: I am the Lord. And the blood shall be to you for a token upon the houses where ye are: and when I see the blood, I will pass over you, and the plague shall not be upon you to destroy you, when I smite the land of Egypt" (Ex. 12:12–13).

The blood on the doorpost was a distinguishing mark. It was a mark of ownership. That blood said, "This house belongs to a child of God." That blood was a symbol of God's ownership of the people in that house. It is still the same thing for us. When we are saved, we pass under the blood. And when we are saved by the blood, that blood is a distinguishing mark upon us. God's ownership passes upon us. We are not our own. We belong to him.

That blood in Egypt meant that that household was spared from the death that was coming. So for us who have received Jesus Christ as our Savior, the blood means that we have been redeemed. The blood means that we do not belong to the kingdom of darkness, that we will not experience the second death. We have been redeemed, and that redemption is our personal possession.

That blood in Egypt was a mark of love. It demonstrated God's love for his people. The blood today represents God's love for us. When we look at the cross and see the shed blood of Jesus Christ upon that cross, we see a vivid picture of God's love for us. That love is unlimited. "He that spared not his own Son, but delivered him up for us all, how shall he not with him also freely give us all things?" (Rom. 8:32). His love is an unlimited and unqualified love.

We who have entered into a blood-bought relationship with Jesus Christ have received a unique salvation. It is complete in itself. We need nothing else. It is a costly salvation. It is a salvation that has a purpose. It is a salvation that is eternal. It is a salvation that marks us as belonging to God, that shows we have been redeemed, that we are objects of his love. Without the shedding of his blood, there is no forgiveness of sin. We are saved by his death. His shed blood was God's provision for our sins.

15
Temptation

We have all had many encounters with temptation. I used to think that when I got older and more mature, temptation would not be so strong. But that is not so. Temptation is stronger today than it ever has been. I am just as prone to fail, to deny God, to sin today as I ever have been. I may work on the flesh, try to improve it, psych it up, educate it, and add social graces to all of the things that are a part of my human makeup; but when I have done all of that, it still is flesh. "So then they that are in the flesh cannot please God" (Rom. 8:8). When I have done everything I can do, temptation is still real. I wish I could say that when we reach a certain milestone in our lives, it will be easier for us to face Satan and temptation. But that is not so. Temptation grows more severe with the passing of time. The closer we get to God, the stronger and more subtle temptations are.

There are three positions that we can take regarding temptation. First of all, we can accept the situation as it is and be content to live a life of failure and defeat. Many folks do that. Their favorite saying is "Grin and bear it." Thinking there is nothing they can do about defeat, they just accept it.

There is a second position we can take. We can struggle with temptation, resist it, and learn mental and psychological gimmicks and tricks to pull on ourselves. That is probably a better choice than the first one. We will know some victory because we will come up with something that will help us for a while.

The best position is to turn to God's Word for the answer and have victory. God does not want us to be defeated by temptation.

Temptation is the inducement to sin. It is an incitement to sin that comes from outside of us. It plays upon our nature and causes us to consider sin. Sin comes as a result of temptation, but temptation is not the cause of sin. The cause of sin is the will of the individual. Temptation influences my will, but it does not determine my will. Flip Wilson made it popular to say, "The devil made me do it." However, that is not so. He may influence us, and he may try to get us to do some things, but ultimately the cause of sin is our own choice, our own will. Temptation cannot force us to sin. Man sins when he is enticed and led astray by his own lust (Jas. 1:14). We sin because we choose to sin. Temptation prods us along and makes it easy to do what we choose to do, but it is not the cause of sin. Every temptation of Satan is for the purpose of destroying our hope for fulfillment, satisfaction, and peace.

Let us examine two passages of Scripture. "There hath no temptation taken you but such as is common to man: but God is faithful, who will not suffer you to be tempted above that ye are able . . . to bear it"(1 Cor. 10:13). "Let no man say when he is tempted, I am tempted of God: for God cannot be tempted with evil, neither tempteth he any man: But every man is tempted, when he is drawn away of his own lust, and enticed" (James 1:13–14).

The Source of Temptation

God may test us through temptation, but God does not tempt us to do evil. That is against God's nature. God cannot be tempted because God's nature is one of absolute holiness. Temptation is only effective if there is inside the person who is tempted a weakness or a desire to sin. God has no such desire, no such weakness. His character is holy and righteous. God cannot be tempted; and, because of that, he does not tempt us. Satan never tempts us to do anything that we do not make it easy for him to do. Every man is tempted by the pull of his own desires.

Temptation does not come from God but from Satan. We have residing in us a sinful nature. Lust resides there. But temptation comes from without. The apostle Paul encourages faithfulness by husband and wife in the physical relationship of marriage. Physical relationship in marriage ought to be shared in love so that Satan will not have an occasion to tempt us.

The temptation to sin is the temptation to abuse good. We have misunderstood temptation. We have thought that temptation was an encouragement to do something bad, something wrong. There is a degree in which that is true; but, more accurately, temptation is an encouragement to do something normal and proper in the wrong way. Everything that God gave us is good. Sin is the perversion of good. Immorality is to take good, which was created for us by God, and to use it in the wrong way, in the wrong context, for the wrong purpose.

We can see this clearly if we look at the first temptation in the Bible. "When the woman saw that the tree was good for food, and that it was pleasant to the eyes, and a tree to be desired to make one wise, she took of the fruit thereof, and did eat, and gave also unto her husband with her; and he did eat" (Gen. 3:6). Eve was tempted at the point of some very normal and very proper desires and needs. She was tempted at the point of physical appetite. The tree was good for food. There is nothing wrong in taking care of our physical appetites. The wrong was satisfying physical appetite by doing what God had forbidden. The desire was normal and natural, but the way it was fulfilled was not proper and thus was sinful.

Further, the tree was pleasant to the eyes. It appealed to her sense of the beautiful. There is nothing wrong with beauty. If we did not have an eye for beautiful things, it would not mean a thing for us to read about the beauties in heaven, about the glories of the new Jerusalem, and about all the beautiful sights that God has prepared for us. The sense of the beautiful and that which is lovely is a normal, natural, healthy, wholesome desire. She abused that sense of beauty.

The tree was desirable to make her wise. It is not wrong to desire knowledge. That is a healthy desire. There should be a hunger in our hearts for knowledge. But she sought to fulfill that desire for knowledge in disobedience and rebellion against God. Temptation may appeal to the best that is in us, and it may endeavor to get us to satisfy a normal desire in the wrong way.

The deeper we become spiritually, the more subtle and stronger are the attacks of Satan. None of us can ever get to the place where we are confident in our own strength in the face of temptation. When we think we are strong, we are one step away from disaster. Even a godly minister is prone to sin. The stronger we get spiritually, the subtler and stronger is the attack of temptation.

All over America today there are men who have held strong and powerful positions, who have had a voice in shaping the theological thought of America, and yet have fallen victim to dishonesty, impurity, or some other sin that they thought they were exempt from. The closer we get to God, the more we must depend upon God for our every need in the face of temptation.

"For all that is in the world, the lust of the flesh, and the lust of the eyes, and the pride of life, is not of the Father, but is of the world" (1 John 2:16). We need to underline this in our Bibles because if we could understand this verse, we would learn something that would protect us the rest of our lives. This is the devil's secret. If we will take it to heart, we will be armed and fully warned against the attacks of Satan.

Here we have the three basic ingredients to every temptation. The lust of the flesh is a consuming passion to do. The lust of the eyes is a consuming passion to have. The pride of life is a consuming passion to be. Every temptation comes in one of those three areas. Satan tempts us at the point of something we want to do, something we want to have, or something we want to be. He has never varied his attack from the very first time with Eve in the garden. His own rebellion against God (Isa. 14) follows this pattern. Even the temptations of Jesus fit this approach.

Look at Isaiah 14 in the rebellion of Lucifer. "Thou hast said in thine heart, I will ascend into heaven [there is the lust of the flesh, the compulsion to do], I will exalt my throne above the stars of God [that is the compulsion to have] . . . I will be like the most High [that is the compulsion to be]" (Isa. 14:13–14). This is the approach Satan always makes to us. If we yield to temptation today, Satan will take us down the path exactly as we have seen. We will do it in full knowledge with full understanding. He is not going to trick us. He is going to approach us in at least one of these ways.

The System of Temptation

Now look at the system of temptation. How will Satan tempt us? We have already given the ingredients of temptation, but what is his approach to it? It is very simple. In Genesis 3 we can trace it clearly. "The serpent was more subtil than any beast of the field which the Lord God made. And he said unto the woman, Yea, hath God said, Ye shall not eat of every tree of the garden?" (Gen. 3:1). He cast doubt on God's word. He did not come right out and say, "God is lying to you." What he said was, "Did God really say that?" It is a very innocent question designed to raise doubt.

When doubt was not repulsed, he moved in further. "The serpent said unto the woman, Ye shall not surely die" (Gen. 3:4). He led her to doubt God's word; and when she allowed that doubt a place to grow in her heart, he moved in with an outright lie. "You won't die." But she did die. Every cemetery, every funeral, and every tear of grief in this world is the result of man believing the lie of Satan. That is the way Satan works today.

Perhaps he comes into a home and finds children who have a tendency to be rebellious against their parents. Satan convinces them that God did not really mean it when he said for us to obey our parents. He leads them through a lack of respect, through a lack of Christian commitment, to disobey God, on the premise that it will not make any difference. Thus, he leads us to sow seeds that will come back to us in a bitter harvest.

The first recorded use of the word of God in the Bible was to doubt its accuracy and to deny its truth. It is mentioned by Satan with the purpose of causing Eve to doubt God's word. Satan has presented the same lie down through the years.

Satan continues and makes a wonderful offer: "For God doth know that in the day ye eat thereof, then your eyes shall be opened, and ye shall be as gods, knowing good and evil" (Gen. 3:5). He used the name of God to foster his temptation. He implied that God was cheating Eve.

God does not cheat us. He is trying to protect us. Anything God does not want us to have, we do not want. We may think we do, but we do not want it because everything that is not of faith and trust is sin. And the wages of sin is death. Anything we take despite God's not wanting us to have it will end in spiritual anguish and unhappiness.

Satan came to Eve with one of the most subtle temptations of all. It is so relevant for us today. He basically said, "You will be as God. You will know good and evil." He mentioned good and evil in the same breath as though they had equal value. He was saying, "You don't appreciate good until you know evil." He mentioned good and evil in such a way as to imply that they have equal desirability and equal value.

Nothing could be further from the truth. We do not have to eat out of a garbage can to know that it is garbage. We do not have to have open heart surgery to perform open heart surgery. We do not have to have a divorce to counsel people who are considering a divorce. That is a lie from Satan. That is one of the ways he tempts us.

The most tragic reasoning in the world occurs when we fall for that line. He has never changed his tactics. There are more broken and ruined lives because of people's swallowing that line from Satan than we could possibly know. Every one of us has more experience with that failure than we want to admit. One thing is for sure: On our own, we cannot defeat temptation. We need to respect the snares of Satan. We are not capable of facing them alone. Satan is more powerful than we are.

The Success Over Temptation

There is one other thing that we must consider. That is how to have success over temptation. To discover the answer we must look at the example of Jesus. Jesus gives us the perfect pattern for dealing with temptation. In Matthew 4 is recorded three encounters that Jesus had with temptation. When we read carefully Luke 8 and Hebrews 4:15, we find that Jesus was tempted in all ways as we are. He faced every possible temptation. Some say that Jesus was different, that he could not sin. Certainly he had no sinful nature. There was no lust within him that cried out for sin, but the temptation of Jesus was a severe temptation. It was even more severe than the temptations we experience because temptation is such an agony to holiness.

The writer of Hebrews spoke about Jesus suffering under temptation. We do not always suffer under it. We enjoy it sometimes. But because of Jesus' perfect holiness, the temptation to sin had to cause his heart to turn within him and to cringe and ache, for the holiness of God was being confronted with the temptation of Satan. His temptations were real and genuine. Through his temptations he told us how we can have victory over temptation.

"Then was Jesus led up of the Spirit into the wilderness to be tempted of the devil. And when he had fasted forty days and forty nights, he was afterward an hungered. And when the tempter came to him, he said, If thou be the Son of God, command that these stones be made bread. But he answered and said, It is written, Man shall not live by bread alone, but by every word that proceedeth out of the mouth of God" (Matt. 4:1–4). He was asking Jesus to compromise and not to trust God by using his own power to turn stones into bread. It was the temptation to Jesus to do something that was displeasing to God.

"Then the devil taketh him up into the holy city, and setteth him on a pinnacle of the temple, And saith unto him, If thou be the Son of God, cast thyself down: for it is written, He shall give his angels charge concerning thee: and in their hands they shall bear thee up, lest at any time thou dash thy foot against a stone" (Matt. 4:5–6). This was the temptation for Jesus to cast himself from the pinnacle of the temple in a spectacular display and let the angels catch him and safely escort him to the ground. With that display the people would accept him. Here was the temptation to have the acclaim of the people in a cheap way. It was the temptation of the lust of the eyes.

"Again, the devil taketh him up into an exceeding high mountain, and sheweth him all the kingdoms of the world, and the glory of them; And saith unto him, All these things will I give thee, if thou wilt fall down and worhip me" (Matt. 4:8–9). This temptation was at the point of the consuming desire to be.

Jesus faced all of these temptations. He faced the same pattern that we face. But, with each one, notice what he says: "It is written" (Matt. 4:4,7,10). How do we have victory over temptation? By putting the Word of God into our hearts. We put our trust and our faith in the principles of the Bible and base our lives upon it. It becomes our rule of practice. The psalmist said: "Thy word have I hid in mine heart, that I might not sin against thee" (Ps. 119:11). It was the hidden Word inside the heart of Jesus that allowed him to combat Satan and have victory over temptation.

The last portion of verse 10 gives us a tremendous truth. "For it is written, Thou shalt worship the Lord thy God, and him only shalt thou serve" (Matt. 4:10). Here is a tremendous truth. Worship and service go together. We will serve whoever we worship. If we are not serving God, that tells us that we are not worshiping God. If we worship God, we will serve God. Worship and service go together.

It is not a sin to be tempted. Many times we have tremendous guilt because we are tempted. We will be tempted. I have had the experience of reading the Bible and all of a sudden a blasphemous thought would come into my mind. I have had the experience of witnessing to someone in a home, and all of a sudden a lustful thought would come into my mind. We have all been tempted.

In talking about our great High Priest who is making reconciliation for the sins of the people, the writer of Hebrews said, "Since he himself has now been through suffering and temptation, he knows what it is like when we suffer and are tempted, and he is wonderfully able to help us" (Heb. 2:18, TLB). "This High Priest of ours understands our weaknesses, since he had the same temptations we do, though he never once gave way to them and sinned" (Heb. 4:15, TLB). It is not a sin to be tempted. The sin comes when we give temptation a place in our lives, when we do not immediately bring the Word of God to rebuke the temptor in God's power, allowing God to give us victory.

Temptation is real. In the latter days, as history moves toward a climax, wickedness will increase and temptation will grow stronger. If there was ever a time when there needed to be a pure church, when there needed to be a people who will march into the face of temptation in his strength, it is today!

16
The Security of the Believer

The Bible indicates that salvation is a work of God's grace. It is given to an individual upon his willingness to receive it, demonstrated by his repentance and faith. It is not contingent upon his personal merit or value. God is the one who saves the person and who keeps the person saved.

"Because of what Christ did, all you others too, who heard the Good News about how to be saved, and trusted Christ, were marked as belonging to Christ by the Holy Spirit, who long ago had been promised to all of us Christians. His presence within us is God's guarantee that he really will give us all that he promised; and the Spirit's seal upon us means that God has already purchased us and that he guarantees to bring us to himself. This is just one more reason for us to praise our glorious God" (Eph. 1:13–14, TLB).

The doctrine of eternal security maintains that when a person is once saved, he can never stop being saved. There are two strong bases for this doctrine.

The Nature of Redemption

If we are to understand what the Bible says about security, we need first to examine what salvation really is. Salvation is not a doctrine, creed, or theological premise. It is a person. When we speak of losing salvation, we are not talking about losing a particular theological position, a certain spiritual commitment; we are discussing losing a person, Jesus Christ. Salvation is in the person of Jesus Chrsit. "This is the record, that God has given to us eternal life, and this life is in his son. He that hath the Son hath life; and he that hath not the Son of God hath not life" (1 John 5:11–12).

Eternal life is in Jesus Christ, and one cannot have salvation without having Jesus. If one does not have Jesus, he does not have salvation. "Verily, verily, I say unto you, The hour is coming, and now is, when the dead shall hear the voice of the Son of God: and they that hear shall live. For as the Father hath life in himself; so hath he given to the Son to have life in himself" (John 5:25–26). Eternal life *is* Jesus Christ.

The apostle Paul spoke of the gospel as the power of God "Who hath saved us, and called us with an holy calling, not according to our works, but according to his own purpose and grace, which was given us in Christ Jesus before the world began, But is now made manifest by the appearing of our Saviour Jesus Christ, who hath abolished death, and hath brought life and immortality to light through the gospel. For the which cause I also suffer these things: nevertheless I am not ashamed: for I know whom I have believed, and am persuaded that he is able to keep that which I have committed unto him against that day" (2 Tim. 1:9–10,12). It does not say "in whom"; it says "whom." It is not "I know what I have believed." It is "whom I have believed." We may not understand all the deep doctrines of the Word of God, but we can know Jesus Christ. Salvation is a person— Jesus Christ.

Second, salvation is a free gift that we receive by faith. "But God, who is rich in mercy, for his great love wherewith he loved us, Even when we were dead in sins, hath quickened us together with Christ (by grace ye are saved); And hath raised us up together, and made us sit together in heavenly places in Christ Jesus: That in the ages to come he might shew the exceeding riches of his grace in his kindness toward us through Christ Jesus. For by grace are ye saved through faith; and that not of yourselves: it is the gift of God: Not of works, lest any man should boast. For we are his workmanship, created in Christ Jesus unto good works, which God hath before ordained that we should walk in them" (Eph. 2:4–10).

In the second part of Romans 6:23 Paul declared that "the gift of God is eternal life through Jesus Christ our Lord." And read again the familiar passage we all have learned: "For God so loved the world, that he gave his only begotten Son, that whosoever believeth in him should not perish, but have everlasting life. He that believeth on him is not condemned: but he that believeth not is condemned already, because he hath not believed in the name of the only begotten Son of God" (John 3:16,18).

"He that believeth on the Son hath everlasting life: and he that believeth not the Son shall not see life; but the wrath of God abideth on him" (John 3:36). We must understand what salvation is before we talk about whether we can lose salvation. Salvation is a relationship with Jesus Christ. He loves me in spite of my sin. He reaches down to me even though I am unworthy of his attention. His love touches my life. "We love him, because he first loved us" (1 John 4:19).

His love initiates contact with my soul and draws me to himself. I embrace him through faith and receive Christ as my personal Savior. I am not saved because I believe a certain doctrinal fact or because I belong to a certain church. I am not saved because I have been initiated by certain rites in a religious organization. I am saved through personal faith in Jesus Christ.

The Nature of Divine Activity

The second basis for the security of the believer is the nature of divine activity.

First of all, examine the divine activity of God. God keeps and God secures! "I know this, that whatever God does is final—nothing can be added or taken from it; God's purpose in this is that man should fear the all-powerful God. Whatever is, has been long ago; and whatever is going to be has been before; God brings to pass again what was in the distant past and disappeared" (Eccl. 3:14–15, TLB). When God does something, it stands done and can never be undone. It is so firmly done that God, before the foundation of the world, knew those who would respond to him, and he foreordained them to be saved because he knew their response. The fact that they are going to be saved and be in glory is as unchangeable as past history.

It is no surprise to God when one is saved. God knew it before the individual was ever born. God foreordained it. Paul spoke about God, saying that "whom he did foreknow, he did predestinate" (Rom. 8:29). God's predestination is based upon his foreknowledge, and God knew every person who would be saved before this world was ever begun. When God does something, he does it forever! When he does it, the future is just as certain as the past. God is the one who keeps us.

"I am leaving the world, and leaving them behind, and coming to you. Holy Father, keep them in your own care— all those you have given me—so that they will be united just as we are, with none missing. During my time here I have kept safe within your family all of these you gave me. I guarded them so that not one perished, except the son of hell, as the Scriptures foretold. I'm not asking you to take them out of the world, but to keep them safe from Satan's power. I am not praying for these alone but also for the future believers who will come to me because of the testimony of these" (John 17:11–12,15,20, TLB). Jesus here thanked God that he had kept everyone who was saved. Not one had been lost.

"My sheep hear my voice, and I know them, and they follow me: And I give unto them eternal life; and they shall never perish" (John 10:27). He said they will *never* perish. If one person ever was saved and then became lost, Jesus is a liar. Jesus said that they will never perish. "Neither shall any man pluck them out of my hand. My Father, which gave them me, is greater than all; and no man is able to pluck them out of my Father's hand. I and my Father are one" (John 10:28–30). The word *pluck* is a Greek word that means to take away by force. We are held in his hand, and nothing has the power to take us out of Christ's hand.

"For the gifts and calling of God are without repentance" (Rom. 11:29). The gifts that God gives and the calling that he extends are unchanging.

"And now—all glory to him who alone is God, who saves us through Jesus Christ our Lord; yes, splendor and majesty, all power and authority are his from the beginning; his they are and his they evermore shall be. And he is able to keep you from slipping and falling away, and to bring you, sinless and perfect, into his glorious presence with mighty shouts of everlasting joy" (Jude 24–25, TLB). "All that the Father giveth me shall come to me; and him that cometh to me I will in no wise cast out" (John 6:37). "Even when we are too weak to have any faith left, he remains faithful to us and will help us, for he cannot disown us who are part of himself, and he will always carry out his promises to us" (2 Tim. 2:13, TLB). If we are unfaithful, God is still faithful. The key to security is not our faithfulness, but God's faithfulness.

Our salvation is based upon an agreement between God and Jesus Christ. Jesus Christ, the Son of God, agreed to pay the debt for our sins upon the cross. He was the perfect, sinless, virgin-born Son of God. When he died upon that cross, he was the perfect sacrifice for our sins. He was also the perfect high priest. When he died, he went into the holy of holies in heaven taking his own precious blood, and there he was both sacrifice and priest. He offered an eternal sacrifice upon the holy of holies in heaven for us. It is his saving work that is done and stands done. It is his faithfulness that we are counting on. We may deny him, but he cannot deny himself.

Christians are those who have been saved. "God has reserved for his children the priceless gift of eternal life; it is kept in heaven for you, pure and undefiled, beyond the reach of change and decay. And God, in his mighty power, will make sure that you get there safely to receive it, because you are trusting him. It will be yours in that coming last day for all to see" (1 Pet. 1:4–5, TLB). We are kept for our inheritance in heaven through the power of God, and it will be revealed in the last time.

"I am sure that God who began the good work within you will keep right on helping you grow in his grace until his task within you is finally finished on that day when Jesus Christ returns" (Phil. 1:6, TLB). We did not start salvation—God did. When God starts something, he finishes it. A born-again believer will persevere to the end, but it will be because God perseveres through him. Salvation, from its beginning on this earth until it is consummated in glory, is the work of God. Salvation is the product of divine activity. It is not human effort. God keeps and God secures.

Secondly, Christ intercedes for us. Christ is our advocate who pleads our case before God. "My little children, I am telling you this so that you will stay away from sin. But if you sin, there is someone to plead for you before the Father. His name is Jesus Christ, the one who is all that is good and who pleases God completely" (1 John 2:1, TLB). While God is securing us and keeping us, Jesus Christ is pleading our case. Jesus Christ is standing beside us. Jesus Christ is our advocate. He is pleading our cause before the throne of grace. When we voice prayers that do not seem to make sense, Jesus is there interceding, interpreting, and making sure that every concern of our hearts is properly interpreted before the throne of God.

If it were up to us to defend ourselves, we would be in trouble because we never have a valid excuse for our sin. Our sin is irrational. It is always against our best interests. If we had to defend it before God, we would have no defense at all. So when we sin and the devil accuses us before God, Jesus steps in and says, "Now wait a minute. His sins are under the blood. I died for his sins." Satan has no power over him. Satan has no authority over him. That sin is cleansed and forgiven.

The book of Jude begins, "Jude, the servant of Jesus Christ, and brother of James, to them that are sanctified by God the Father, and preserved in Jesus Christ" (Jude 1). We are preserved in Christ. The writer of Hebrews revealed that Jesus "is able also to save them to the uttermost that come unto God by him, seeing he ever liveth to make intercession for them" (Heb. 7:25). When we are saved, we gain an advocate. He said, "I will never leave thee, nor forsake thee"

(Heb. 13:5). We are secured not by our determination but by the eternal activity of God through his Son, Jesus Christ. Wherever we go, God goes with us. God preserves and keeps us.

Third, the Holy Spirit works in us. The work of the Holy Spirit is to seal the believer. "Ye were sealed with that Holy Spirit of promise" (Eph. 1:13). The moment that we are saved, we are immediately joined to God in an eternal relationship. We are *sealed* with the Holy Spirit. This means two things. The first is that God seals or brands us. "It is this God who has made you and me into faithful Christians and commissioned us apostles to preach the Good News. He has put his brand upon us—his mark of ownership—and given us his Holy Spirit in our hearts as guarantee that we belong to him, and as the first installment of all that he is going to give us" (2 Cor. 1:21–22, TLB). The second aspect of this is that we are sealed with the Spirit. God is the one who seals, and the Holy Spirit is the seal.

The seal was used to permanently mark something. The word *seal* is used to describe the impression that is put on copper with a hammer. When we look at a coin, we find impressions on both sides of the coin. Those impressions are made by a seal that imprints those coins. That is the word that is used in this Scripture. There is a sealing, a marking that takes place.

The seal comes following personal commitment. God does not force his way on anyone. Nobody has to be saved. There will come a time when those who have not bowed their knees to Christ will be forced to do it when Jesus returns, but they will not be saved. It will be too late for them. They will be assigned their destination in hell. "In whom ye also trusted, after that ye heard the word of truth, the gospel of your salvation" (Eph. 1:13). We trusted Christ when we heard the gospel preached. The sealing of the Holy Spirit takes place after the trusting, after we give our hearts to Christ. So a personal commitment is involved.

Secondly, the sealing takes place at conversion. It is not something that happens later down the line. When we were saved, we were sealed. "After that ye heard" and "after that ye believed" should be translated, "Upon hearing, you trusted; and upon believing, you were sealed." These phrases indicate that the sealing takes place at the same time the believing does. Sealing takes place at the point of conversion.

The idea of the seal is that the transaction is completed. That means that we have been bought. "God has bought you with a great price. So use every part of your body to give glory back to God, because he owns it" (1 Cor. 6:20, TLB). When we were sealed, the transaction was completed. An exchange of ownership has taken place. Throughout the epistles Paul called himself a slave. The word *doulos*, which is translated *slave*, means a servitude that can only be broken by death. The only way we can get out of that slavery is either for us to die or for our master to die.

Before we were saved, we served Satan. He was our master. But we died. We died with Jesus Christ. When we died, we passed out of the servitude of Satan. By our death, we were freed from him. Now we are bound to Jesus Christ. The only way we can get out of that servitude is for us to die or for him to die. Jesus said, "Whosoever liveth and believeth in me shall never die" (John 11:26); and Jesus, being God, never dies. Thus we can never stop being a slave of Jesus Christ. We are bound to him. We are sealed. We may not always live as though we belong to him, but his mark is still indelibly upon us. We cannot sin and find lasting pleasure in it. Our hearts smite us. We cannot get away from that. We have become his personal possessions.

"I pray that your hearts will be flooded with light so that you can see something of the future he has called you to share. I want you to realize that God has been made rich because we who are Christ's have been given to him!" (Eph. 1:18, TLB). We are his inheritance, and the inheritance of Christ cannot be changed.

The Jews would understand it because one of the procedures in the Jewish sacrificial system was for the priest to examine carefully for any physical blemish the lambs that were available for sacrifice. When the lamb that was perfect had been picked out, it was sealed with the seal of the Temple itself. That seal meant that the lamb now belonged to God. That lamb had been set apart for the purposes of God.

The seal was permanent. It was always intended to be. When Jesus died and was placed in the tomb, the seal of the Roman Empire was placed on it. That seal demanded that it never be opened. In reality, man does not have the power to enforce a permanency like that. Man can try to make something permanent, but he cannot do it. God has the power to do it. Man may have the will to do it, but he does not have the power to carry through. But God does! When God seals something, it stays sealed. It is a permanent sealing.

That sealing is just a foretaste, a down payment. It is called "the earnest of our inheritance" (Eph. 1:14). When we become Christians, God plants his Spirit in us. He plants his nature in us. Earnest money is applied toward the total principle, but it is paid in advance. God is going to take us through to the full inheritance. He inherits us. We inherit him.

To be sure, the Bible indicates that we are to persevere

to the end. But remember, God works in us, both to will and to do (Phil. 2:13). God keeps us from falling. God does a work in us that shall never change. It is forever! The past? The future? It is all certain because it is all in the purpose and plan of God.

17
The Meaning of Forgiveness

One of the most beautiful doctrines of the Christian faith is that of forgiveness. The Christian message is called the gospel. *Gospel* means "good news." The good news is that man can be forgiven. Forgiveness is a cherished possession. It is something that happens at the time of salvation, but it is also a continuing possession of the child of God.

The word *forgiveness* is not a uniquely religious term. *Forgive* is used in secular life, but it has special significance to those of us who have come to know Jesus Christ as our personal Savior. He has given us forgiveness of sins.

"They shall teach no more every man his neighbour, and every man his brother, saying, Know the Lord: for they shall all know me, from the least of them unto the greatest of them, saith the Lord: *for I will forgive their iniquity, and I will remember their sin no more*" (Jer. 31:34).

"Bless the Lord, O my soul: and all that is within me, bless his holy name. Bless the Lord, O my soul, and forget not all his benefits: Who forgiveth all thine iniquities; who healeth all thy diseases; Who redeemeth thy life from destruction; who crowneth thee with lovingkindness and tender mercies; who satisfieth thy mouth with good things; so that thy youth is renewed like the eagle's. The Lord is merciful and gracious, slow to anger, and plenteous in mercy. He will not always chide: neither will he keep his anger for ever. He hath not dealt with us after our sins; nor rewarded us according to our iniquities. For as the heaven is high above the earth, so great is his mercy toward them that fear him. As far as the east is from the west, so far hath he removed our transgressions from us. Like as a father pitieth his children, so the Lord pitieth them that fear him" (Ps. 103:1–5,8–13).

Isaiah spoke of the hypocrisy of religious activity without a deep, personal commitment to God. He commanded the people to repent and to turn to God. To climax the message he said, "Come now, and let us reason together, saith the Lord: though your sins be as scarlet, they shall be as white as snow; though they be red like crimson, they shall be as wool" (Isa. 1:18).

These verses are just the tip of the iceberg, just a few of literally hundreds of verses in the Bible dealing with the subject of forgiveness.

The Reason for Forgiveness

There are two basic reasons why forgiveness is important to us and why we as individuals need forgiveness. The first reason is guilt! Man feels guilty because he is guilty. Man is a rebel against God. Because of guilt we desperately need forgiveness. The Word of God declares: "O Lord, have mercy on me in my anguish. My eyes are red from weeping; my health is broken from sorrow. I am pining away with grief; my years are shortened, drained away because of sadness. My sins have sapped my strength; I stoop with sorrow and with shame" (Ps. 31:9–10, TLB).

The psalmist continued: "O Lord, don't punish me while you are angry! Your arrows have struck deep; your blows are crushing me. Because of your anger my body is sick, my health is broken beneath my sins. They are like a flood, higher than my head; they are a burden too heavy to bear. My wounds are festering and full of pus. Because of my sins I am bent and racked with pain. My days are filled with anguish. My loins burn with inflammation and my whole body is diseased. I am exhausted and crushed; I groan in despair. Lord, you know how I long for my health once more. You hear my every sigh. My heart beats wildly, my strength fails, and I am going blind" (Ps. 38:1–10, TLB).

This is a tremendous description of what sin does in our lives and the guilt that it brings into our experience. We are being told today that we need to adjust ourselves to our guilt. But the Bible says that we need our guilt removed. We do not need to get used to it; we need to get rid of it.

Second, we need forgiveness because of our sin. We are guilty because we are sinners. Sin is against God; thus, sin can only be forgiven by God. Forgiveness is the only solution for sin. Every one of us has sinned. We have "all . . . come short of the glory of God" (Rom. 3:23). Our sin is against God. David cried out after he had been rebuked because of his sin: "Against thee, thee only, have I sinned" (Ps. 51:4). His sin affected Uriah and the nation of Israel. It affected his place as king and priest in the nation. But it was basically against God. Sin is an attack on God. It is an assault upon God. Since only God can deal with sin, forgiveness is necessary. We must have forgiveness because of the reality of sin in our lives.

That is man's side. The reason for forgiveness is because of our guilt and our sin. But from God's side, what is the reason for forgiveness? There are two reasons that are very closely related. One is God's love. He forgives us because he loves us.

When God was explaining to the people why he was going to keep his promises to them, he declared: "You are a holy people, dedicated to the Lord your God. He has chosen you from all the people on the face of the whole earth to be his own chosen ones. He didn't choose you and pour out his love upon you because you were a larger nation than any other, for you were the smallest of all! It was just because he loves you, and because he kept his promise to your ancestors. . . . Understand, therefore, that the Lord your God is the faithful God who for a thousand generations keeps his promises and constantly loves those who love him and who obey his commands" (Deut. 7:6–9, TLB).

There is no reason for God to forgive us except that he loves us. He does not have to forgive us because of anything we have done. He forgives us because he loves us. His heart is filled with compassion for us, and he responds to our need because he loves us.

The other side of that, and very closely connected to it, is grace. We need to be forgiven. Because he loves us, he moves in grace to save us. Not one thing do we add to God's grace. His grace brings us into relationship with him. It is his grace that brings salvation to us. We are saved not because of our merit but because God does something for us that we do not deserve. That is grace, and that is God's side in this matter of forgiveness.

"God says he will accept and acquit us—declare us 'not guilty'—if we trust Jesus Christ to take away our sins. And we all can be saved in this same way, by coming to Christ, no matter who we are or what we have been like. Yes, all have sinned; all fall short of God's glorious ideal; yet now God declares us 'not guilty' of offending him if we trust in Jesus Christ, who in his kindness freely takes away our sins. For God sent Christ Jesus to take the punishment for our sins and to end all God's anger against us. He used Christ's blood and our faith as the means of saving us from his wrath.

In this way he was being entirely fair, even though he did not punish those who sinned in former times. For he was looking forward to the time when Christ would come and take away those sins" (Rom. 3:22–25, TLB). From the divine side, God brings forgiveness based upon his grace. His love, prompted and empowered by grace, brings salvation to those who will receive it.

The Requirements for Forgiveness

Let us look at the requirements for forgiveness. Forgiveness is something that has certain conditions attached to it. We are not forgiven just because we love Jesus. We are not forgiven just because we recognize we have done wrong. There are three basic conditions or requirements that are found in the Word of God.

The first requirement is repentance. Repentance is turning from our sin to God. Repentance means that we turn around, that we change directions. The Greek word for *repentance* means a reorientation of thought. We once loved something; now we hate it. We once hated something; now we love it. We have a new attitude toward God. We have a new attitude toward the world and toward ourselves. Repentance is to turn *from* sin *to* God.

"Seek ye the Lord while he may be found, call ye upon him while he is near: Let the wicked forsake his way, and the unrighteous man his thoughts: and let him return unto the Lord, and he will have mercy upon him; and to our God, for he will abundantly pardon" (Isa. 55:6–7).

"They said, Turn ye again now every one from his evil way, and from the evil of your doings, and dwell in the land that the Lord hath given unto you and to your fathers for ever and ever" (Jer. 25:5).

"From that time Jesus began to preach, and to say, Repent:

for the kingdom of heaven is at hand" (Matt. 4:17).

"When Jesus heard it, he saith unto them, They that are whole have no need of the physician, but they that are sick: I came not to call the righteous, but sinners to repentance" (Mark 2:17).

"And they went out, and preached that men should repent" (Mark 6:12).

If we want to be forgiven, we must repent. There is no such thing as forgiveness without repentance.

The second condition of forgiveness is confession. If we have really turned from our sins, we will confess them to God. "David's heart smote him after that he had numbered the people. And David said unto the Lord, I have sinned greatly in that I have done: and now, I beseech thee, O Lord, take away the iniquity of thy servant; for I have done very foolishly" (2 Sam. 24:10).

And in the Psalms David prayed, "Have mercy upon me, O God, according to thy lovingkindness: according unto the multitude of thy tender mercies blot out my transgressions. Wash me thoroughly from mine iniquity, and cleanse me from my sin. For I acknowledge my transgressions: and my sin is ever before me. Against thee, thee only, have I sinned and done this evil in thy sight: that thou mightest be justified when thou speakest, and be clear when thou judgest. Behold, I was shapen in iniquity, and in sin did my mother conceive me" (Ps. 51:1–5).

"I acknowledged my sin unto thee, and mine iniquity have I not hid. I said, I will confess my transgressions unto the Lord; and thou forgivest the iniquity of my sin" (Ps. 32:5).

"If we say that we have no sin, we deceive ourselves, and the truth is not in us. If we confess our sins, he is faithful and just to forgive us our sins, and to cleanse us from all unrighteousness" (1 John 1:8–9).

Confession is a condition of forgiveness. There are three aspects of confession: (1) the acknowledgment of sin, (2) the acceptance of its guilt, and (3) the acceptance of forgiveness. Many people know they have sinned and tell us they have sinned. But if they do not receive forgiveness, they have not truly confessed. All they have done is to admit something that is not based upon repentance. When we repent, we will confess our sin to God and will receive forgiveness. Simply admitting a wrong is not confession. Confession involves acknowledging sin and its guilt, but it also involves the acceptance of forgiveness for sin.

The third requirement for forgiveness is a forgiving spirit. If we have been forgiven, we will be forgiving persons. If we do not forgive, that is evidence that we have not forgiven.

When Jesus was giving us the model prayer, he told us to pray like this: "Forgive us our debts, as we forgive our debtors. For if ye forgive men their trespasses, your heavenly Father will also forgive you; But if you forgive not men their trespasses, neither will your Father forgive your trespasses" (Matt. 6:12,14–15).

"Then came Peter to him, and said, Lord, how oft shall my brother sin against me, and I forgive him? till seven times? Jesus saith unto him, I say not unto thee, Until seven times: but, Until seventy times seven" (Matt. 18:21–22).

How often shall we forgive each other? Seventy times seven is 490. Jesus was telling us to keep forgiving. There is never to be a limit to our forgiveness. Remember: "Be ye kind one to another, tenderhearted, forgiving one another, even as God for Christ's sake hath forgiven you" (Eph. 4:32). The reason we can keep forgiving each other is because Christ has forgiven us and is continually forgiving us. He is forgiving us; thus, we are forgiving each other.

Immediately, someone asks, "What are the conditions for

me to forgive somebody?" The one condition for us to forgive others is that they ask us to forgive them. That is all. We are not to evaluate their sincerity. If they ask, we are to forgive them. That is the condition.

We are not to harbor grudges or to be suspicious when people come to us for reconciliation. That is a hard teaching. There are many people of whom we are naturally suspicious. But the one condition is that they come and ask for our forgiveness. If we have not forgiven, it is evidence of a lack of forgiveness in our hearts. More than being a requirement for forgiveness, it is an evidence of forgiveness. Instead of saying that we have to have a forgiving spirit to be forgiven, we should say that a forgiving spirit is evidence that we have been forgiven.

The Results of Forgiveness

These results of forgiveness all occur at the same time. They are simply different aspects of the same thing. When we are forgiven, we are pardoned. "Remember not the sins of my youth, nor my transgressions: according to thy mercy remember thou me for thy goodness' sake, O Lord. For thy name's sake, O Lord, pardon mine iniquity; for it is great. Look upon mine affliction and my pain; and forgive all my sins" (Ps. 25:7,11,18). Pardon is the first result of forgiveness. We have been released from the guilt of our sin.

If we think of forgiveness only in the sense of pardon, then we will come to think that all forgiveness really means is that we do not have to be punished for our sin. Forgiveness is much greater than that! The second result of forgiveness helps us see the other side. When we are forgiven, we are cured, healed. *Pardon* is a legal term. *Cure* is a medical term. We are pardoned from the consequences and the punishment of sin, but we are also cured from the disease of sin. We do not need to merely have the guilt of sin removed; we need to have sin removed. When we are forgiven, we are cured. The cancer of sin is removed from us.

Forgiveness also results in reconciliation. "But if we walk in the light, as he is in the light, we have fellowship one with another, and the blood of Jesus Christ his Son cleanseth us from all sin" (1 John 1:7). "Behold, the Lord's hand is not shortened, that it cannot save; neither his ear heavy, that it cannot hear: But your iniquities have separated between you and your God, and your sins have hid his face from you, that he will not hear" (Isa. 59:1–2). When we are forgiven, there is a reconciliation with God. Pure and perfect fellowship with God is restored when we are forgiven.

The next thing that happens is freedom of guilt. "Blessed is he whose transgression is forgiven, whose sin is covered. Blessed is the man unto whom the Lord imputeth not iniquity, and in whose spirit there is no guile" (Ps. 32:1–2). "Saying, Blessed are they whose iniquities are forgiven, and whose sins are covered. Blessed is the man to whom the Lord will not impute sin" (Rom. 4:7–8).

This matter of freedom from guilt is best seen by the fact that there are four Hebrew words in the Old Testament translated *to forgive.* One of the words means to send away. The second one means to lift a burden. The third one means to cover. And the fourth one means to blot out. When we look at all four words together, they define exactly what forgiveness is. Our sins are sent away. The burden or the guilt is lifted. Our sins are covered. They are blotted out.

The fifth result of forgiveness is cleansing or purging. "If we confess our sins, he is faithful and just to forgive us our sins, and cleanse us from all unrighteousness" (1 John 1:9). Sometimes we hear one say, "How can God forgive me when

I can't forgive myself?" When John says God is "faithful and just to forgive us our sins," that is what happens between us and God. In God's sight we are forgiven. Cleansing is what happens in our sight. In our sight we are clean. Thus we no longer need to loathe ourselves. Christ has performed a miracle in our lives. There is purity and wholeness. We have been cleansed. When Isaiah confessed his sin of the lips we read, "Then flew one of the seraphims unto me, having a live coal in his hand, which he had taken with the tongs from off the altar: And he laid it upon my mouth, and said, Lo, this hath touched thy lips; and thine iniquity is taken away, and thy sin purged" (Isa. 6:6–7).

One further thing needs to be said. Forgiveness means forgetting on God's part. "I will forgive their iniquity, and I will remember their sins no more" (Jer. 31:34). The same verse is quoted in Hebrews 8:12 and Hebrews 10:17. When God forgets it, it means that we have been cleansed as if it never happened. The gospel really does mean that we can start over again. We do not have to live on the basis of our past mistakes. When God forgives us, he forgets. He removes our sin from the record. It is covered in the blood. For a Christian to claim the forgiveness of God and live as if he still had the weight of his sin on his shoulders is detestable to God. When we repent and confess our sins and receive his forgiveness, God cleanses us and removes the guilt, giving us new life and new direction.

After we are saved, what does forgiveness mean? The wonder of forgiveness never ceases. It grows in intensity for the Christian. It is the daily discovery that God does not cast us out. It is the daily discovery that God does not turn his back on us, that he does not reject us. We are Christians, but we are still sinners. We are not magically transferred into a world without temptation. Our recurring faults are blessings because they remind me that salvation is born of God and is maintained only by God. Our part is to repent and to confess. God's part is to forgive and to cleanse.

18
The Coming Judgment

Judgment carries with it the idea of responsibility—of accountability. For someone to face judgment means that he has a responsibility that cannot be discharged without giving an account. This type of situation is found throughout the Word of God: "And be sure your sin will find you out" (Num. 32:23). "Be not deceived; God is not mocked: for whatsoever a man soweth, that shall he also reap. For he that soweth to his flesh shall of the flesh reap corruption; but he that soweth to the Spirit shall of the Spirit reap life everlasting" (Gal. 6:7–8). "Behold, the Lord cometh with ten thousands of his saints, To execute judgment upon all, and to convince all that are ungodly among them of all their ungodly deeds which they have ungodly committed, and all of their hard speeches which ungodly sinners have spoken against him" (Jude 14–15).

Judgment is a reality in the Word of God. We cannot even casually read the Word of God without being made aware of judgment. The Bible is a book of warning. It reminds us that we are indeed responsible individuals. We are accountable unto God, and someday we must face judgment.

The writer of Hebrews said: "It is appointed unto men once to die, but after this the judgment: So Christ was once offered to bear the sins of many; and unto them that look for him shall he appear the second time without sin unto salvation" (Heb. 9:27–28). This verse comes in the midst of a tremendous discussion of the priestly sacrifice of our Lord Jesus Christ and of his promise to come again. It is a reminder to us of the judgment that is going to take place.

The Judgment

There is a sense in which judgment is gradual. "If we would judge ourselves, we should not be judged. But when we are judged, we are chastened of the Lord, that we should not be condemned with the world" (1 Cor. 11:31–32). The chastening hand of God upon the believer is a form of God's judgment upon our lives. In that sense, judgment is gradual.

God does not chasten the lost man in the same sense that he chastens the Christian. The lost man is judged also in a gradual way by the deterioration of his life. Sin has inevitable consequences. There is a sense in which sin is its own judge. "The soul that sinneth, it shall die" (Ezek. 18:4). This means more than physical death. There is a spiritual, mental, and emotional death that takes place when a person rebels against God. There is a deterioration of character and a destruction of happiness and peace. All of that is part of the judgmental process now taking place.

There is also a sense in which judgment is past. The judgment of God upon sin was never more apparent than at the cross. When we look at the cross of Jesus Christ, we see the verdict of God against sinful humanity. Christ, who knew no sin, became sin for us that we might be made the righteousness of God through him (2 Cor. 5:21). At the cross we see evidence of God's judgment upon sin. The cross was the judgment of God upon sin and Satan. Jesus Christ was the willing victim for our sin.

"There is therefore now no condemnation to them which

are in Christ Jesus, who walk not after the flesh, but after the Spirit. For the law of the Spirit of life in Christ Jesus hath made me free from the law of sin and death. For what the law could not do, in that it was weak through the flesh, God sending his own Son in the likeness of sinful flesh, and for sin, condemned sin in the flesh" (Rom. 8:1–3). There on the cross, Jesus Christ bore the penalty of our sin, and he paid the price in full. He was judged for our sins.

"Verily, verily, I say unto you, He that heareth my word, and believeth on him that sent me, hath everlasting life, and shall not come into condemnation; but is passed from death unto life" (John 5:24).

Obviously, this is not the whole picture. Judgment has already taken place in the judgment of God upon sin at the cross of Jesus Christ. It is in the process of taking place as God chastens and disciplines the Christian and as sin takes its natural course of destruction. But the Bible further tells us that there is to be a final judgment. The consequences of sin will result in a terminal confrontation. The gradual confrontation and the past confrontation have to come to a climax in a final judgment. This is primarily what I want to discuss in this chapter.

There are at least seven different judgments spoken of in the Word of God. I consider most of them to be unnecessary for our discussion, but there are two that we need to look at as they relate to final judgment.

First, there is a judgment for the believer. "For other foundation can no man lay than that is laid, which is Jesus Christ. Now if any man build upon this foundation gold, silver, precious stones, wood, hay, stubble; Every man's work shall be made manifest: for the day shall declare it, because it shall be revealed by fire; and the fire shall try every man's work of what sort it is. If any man's work abide which he hath built thereupon, he shall receive a reward. If any man's work shall be burned, he shall suffer loss: but he himself shall be saved; yet so as by fire" (1 Cor. 3:11–15).

"We must all appear before the judgment seat of Christ; that every one may receive the things done in his body, according to that he hath done, whether it be good or bad" (2 Cor. 5:10). This is not a destiny-determining judgment. The child of God is saved and does not face judgment for his sin. The judgment of the Christian is not to determine whether he spends eternity in heaven or hell. It is a judgment to determine the rewards that shall be given to the Christian. It is a judgment of the believer's works. There is a final judgment of the believer, the judgment seat of Christ.

Second, there is a judgment of nonbelievers. "I saw a great white throne, and him that sat on it, from whose face the earth and the heaven fled away; and there was found no place for them. And I saw the dead, small and great, stand before God; and the books were opened: and another book was opened, which is the book of life: and the dead were judged out of those things which were written in the books, according to their works. And death and hell were cast into the lake of fire. This is the second death. And whosoever was not found written in the book of life was cast into the lake of fire" (Rev. 20:11–12,15).

Even nonbelievers will be responsible for their works. This is not a destiny-determining judgment either. Their destiny is already determined. When they rejected Christ, they decided where they would spend eternity. This is a judgment of their works, to reveal the degrees of their punishment. I believe that some people will have more rewards than others in heaven, and some will have greater punishment than others in hell.

There is also a judgment of Satan and the angels that takes place at this same time of the great white throne judgment. "The angels which kept not their first estate, but left their own habitation, he hath reserved in everlasting chains under darkness unto the judgment of the great day" (Jude 6). "God did not spare even the angels who sinned, but threw them into hell, chained in gloomy caves and darkness until the judgment day" (2 Pet. 2:4, TLB).

The judgment is gradual, past, and final. It relates to believers and nonbelievers, to Satan and his angels. Notice the evidence that will be presented at these judgments. "Rejoice, O young man, in thy youth; and let thy heart cheer thee in the days of thy youth, and walk in the ways of thine heart, and in the sight of thine eyes: but know thou, that for all these things God will bring thee into judgment. For God shall bring every work into judgment, with every secret thing, whether it be good, or whether it be evil" (Eccl. 11:9,14).

Jesus said, "I say unto you, That every idle word that men shall speak, they shall give account thereof in the day of judgment. For by thy words thou shalt be justified, and by thy words thou shalt be condemned" (Matt. 12:36–37).

Every secret thought of our hearts, every idle, careless word we have spoken we will face in the judgment. "There is nothing covered, that shall not be revealed; neither hid, that shall not be known. Therefore whatsoever ye have spoken in darkness shall be heard in the light; and that which ye have spoken in the ear in closets shall be proclaimed upon the housetops" (Luke 12:2–3).

The evidence that will be presented is an accurate account of our lives, thoughts, words, and deeds. If we could understand that, it would change our lives. Those thoughts we have that no one else knows about will be known. Every flirtation with evil will be revealed. When we stand before God, whether it is the judgment seat of Christ or the great white throne judgment, the evidence that will be presented will be from a book that God is keeping where every thought, intent, and secret of our lives is recorded.

Well, what about the defense? We may say, "Lord, I am not as bad as it seems."

And he says, "Here is the record. Here is the book. Here is the evidence."

"Well, Lord, I did the best that I could, and I really wanted to see people saved."

"But here is the Book" will be the reply. What will the defense be? There will be none because the evidence will be documented, accurate, and indisputable at the judgment.

What will the verdict be? I have an idea the people who get the most rewards will be people we have never heard of, who never had their names in the paper, who never got to preach before a large church. I do not know what the verdict will be, but I know it will be just and fair. It will be accurate.

"Let a man so account of us, as of the ministers of Christ, and stewards of the mysteries of God. Moreover it is required in stewards, that a man be found faithful. But with me it is a very small thing that I should be judged of you, or of man's judgment: yea, I judge not mine own self. For I know nothing by myself; yet am I not hereby justified: but he that judgeth me is the Lord. Therefore judge nothing before the time, until the Lord come, who both will bring to light the hidden things of darkness, and will make manifest the counsels of the hearts: and then shall every man have praise of God" (1 Cor. 4:1–5).

Every man who has given himself to Christ will have the praise of God. His judgment will have been perfectly carried out because God himself will bring it to light. And as it relates to the unbeliever, there is no question that the judgment is just: "Behold, I come quickly; and my reward is with me, to give every man according as his work shall be" (Rev. 22:12).

The Judge

The Bible speaks further to us about the judge. Who is going to be judge? God has entrusted all judgment to his Son, Jesus Christ. "I saw a great white throne and the one who sat upon it, from whose face the earth and sky fled away" (Rev. 20:11, TLB). The Word is speaking of "Jesus Christ, who shall judge the quick and the dead at his appearing and his kingdom; Henceforth there is laid up for me a crown of righteousness, which the Lord, the righteous judge, shall give me at that day" (2 Tim. 4:1,8).

At the great white throne judgment, after we have stood before the judgment seat of Christ, we will become part of the judicial process. We will be set up as judges with Christ. Christ has made us to be princes and kings, to reign with him (Rev. 1:6). We remember that part of reigning and ruling is judgment. So we shall be judges with him. Paul clearly stated this. "Do ye not know that the saints shall judge the world? and if the world shall be judged by you, are ye unworthy to judge the smallest matters?" (1 Cor. 6:2).

That certainly means that we as saints judge the world by our lives. We walk in this world in such a way that good condemns evil. But Paul went on to say, "Know ye not that we shall judge angels? how much more things that pertain to this life?" (1 Cor. 6:3). So the judge is God through Jesus Christ. We shall share that responsibility by his side.

The Judged

Now look at those who will be judged. The Scripture tells us that the lost will be judged. "The kings of the earth, and the great men, and the rich men, and the chief captains, and the mighty men, and every bondman, and every free man, hid themselves in the dens and in the rocks of the mountains; And said to the mountains and rocks, Fall on us, and hide us from the face of him that sitteth on the throne, and from the wrath of the Lamb: For the great day of his wrath is come; and who shall be able to stand?" (Rev. 6:15–17). These are in contrast to that great host whose robes are white, washed in the blood of the Lamb. They have rejected God. They shall be judged. Every man who judges Christ unworthy of his love and faith will stand before him to be judged.

The saved are to be judged also. "None of us liveth to himself, and no man dieth to himself. For whether we live, we live unto the Lord; and whether we die, we die unto the Lord; whether we live therefore, or die, we are the Lord's. For to this end Christ both died, and rose, and revived, that he might be Lord both of the dead and living. But why dost thou judge thy brother? or why dost thou set at nought thy brother? for we shall all stand before the judgment seat of Christ. For it is written, As I live, saith the Lord, every knee shall bow to me, and every tongue shall confess to God. So then every one of us shall give account of himself to God" (Rom. 14:7–12). The saved will be judged.

What are the results? Neither the judgment at the great white throne nor the judgment seat of Christ is a destiny-determining judgment. Those judgments will confirm the decision made on earth by the individual. This will be done by condemnation and punishment of the lost and by rewards for the saved.

At least five crowns may be given to the Christian.

"Blessed is the man that endureth temptation: for when he is tried, he shall receive the crown of life, which the Lord hath promised to them that love him" (Jas. 1:12). "Be thou faithful unto death, and I will give you a crown of life" (Rev. 2:10). The judged who have given themselves in this life to Jesus Christ will receive a crown of life.

"When the chief Shepherd shall appear, ye shall receive a crown of glory that fadeth not away" (1 Pet. 5:4).

"What is our hope, or joy, or crown of rejoicing? Are not even ye in the presence of our Lord Jesus Christ at his coming? For ye are our glory and joy" (1 Thess. 2:19–20). Those who have responded to the claims of Christ through witness will return to us as a beautiful crown of rejoicing. That is a beautiful crown for the soul-winner.

"Henceforth there is laid up for me a crown of righteousness, which the Lord, the righteous judge, shall give me at that day: and not to me only, but unto all them also that love his appearing" (2 Tim. 4:8).

"Every man that striveth for the mastery is temperate in all things. Now they do it to obtain a corruptible crown; but we are incorruptible" (1 Cor. 9:25).

There is the crown of life, the crown of glory, the crown of rejoicing, the crown of righteousness, and the incorruptible crown.

One may say, "I don't want any crowns; I just want to be with Jesus." I want crowns! And so should you. The Bible tells us that when we stand before him we will lay our crowns at his feet because, in reality, they are not ours—they are his. What matters is not what we have done; it is what he has done through us. The crowns we have are not given as a result of our ability and dedication, but because of the availability that we gave to the Lord.

He in turn performed works in us that were not human works, that were not fleshly works of wood, hay, and stubble. Those shall be burned away. But the works that he wrought through us and the works that he produced through us were like gold, silver, and precious stones. When we come to the judgment before him, we find that we receive the crowns of such works.

And when we stand before him, we can never get over the fact that nothing could have been possible had he not done it. Then we will take the crowns from our heads, and we will place them at his feet and join the innumerable hosts of heaven crying, "Worthy is the Lamb to receive glory and praise, and honor and strength. Worthy is the Lamb."

That is why the judgment is significant. That is why we need to guard every word. If all that was important was getting to heaven, everything would be different. We would have the wrong motives and wrong attitudes. We have seen a little of that in the perversion of Christian truth that says a man can be saved and live as he wants to because he is going to heaven. When we are saved, we enter into a relationship with Christ that can never be broken. When we walk with him, he produces through us works that will bless and touch all of mankind. He rewards us with crowns that we lay at his feet and ascribe to his glory when we stand before him.

The judgment? One thing we know is that it will be accurate; it will be searching. "Neither is there any creature that is not manifest in his sight; but all things are naked and opened unto the eyes of him with whom we have to do" (Heb. 4:13). We know it will be an impartial judgment.

"For there is no respect of persons with God" (Rom. 2:11). There will be no partiality at all.

More than that, it is an eternal judgment. When we stand at the judgment of Christ, there will not be an opportunity for us to say, "Lord, give me a little more time." The lost man who stands before him will cry to be hidden from the wrath of the Lamb. He will want more time. The only options we have are occurring right now! Whatever we would do for God must be done now. The judgment is an eternal judgment. There will be no instant replays. It will be final and eternal.

19
The Second Coming

We now face the tremendous truth of the consummation of the ages. We are dealing with the time when Jesus Christ is to be crowned King of kings and Lord of lords. It is the great anticipation and hope of the church. It is the excitement of the Christian's heart. We can sympathize with the beloved apostle John. After he had seen all that God had revealed to him, his prayer was, "Even so, come, Lord Jesus" (22:21).

This will not be a great theological treatment of this subject. We will simply try to understand what the basic teachings of the Word of God are in regard to the second coming.

Jesus Is Coming

First, Jesus *is* coming. The coming of Jesus Christ is at the forefront of the teachings of the Word of God. By far the most predominant theme in the Bible is the return of the Lord Jesus Christ. It is mentioned more than any of the great cardinal truths except salvation, which obviously includes the teachings of the second coming.

The Bible teaches us that the coming of Jesus Christ is a certainty. "It was not long afterwards that he rose into the sky and disappeared into a cloud, leaving them staring after him. As they were straining their eyes for another glimpse, suddenly two white-robed men were standing there among them, and said, 'Men of Galilee, why are you standing here staring at the sky? Jesus has gone away to heaven, and some day, just as he went, he will return " (Acts 1:9–11, TLB).

The heavenly messengers stood by the disciples and asked them why they were gazing off into the heavens. That is a good question for us today. Anytime we find people preoccupied with the second coming to the extent that they are star gazing instead of doing the task God has assigned them to do, they need to be sobered and brought back down to the earth with the question: "Why are you gazing into heaven?"

Throughout the Word of God is the tremendous truth of the certainty of the coming again of Jesus Christ. The Bible has a way of proving itself. God's messenger warned that a flood would come, and it did. The Bible told us that Jesus would come the first time, and he did. Now the Bible tells us that he will come the second time, and he will! There is a certainty of his return.

His coming will be personal. Jesus himself will come (1 Thess. 4:16). The Lord Jesus Christ whom we long to see, the one who has redeemed us and saved us, will come. Jesus said, "I go to prepare a place for you. And if I go and prepare a place for you, I will come again, and receive you unto myself; that where I am, there ye may be also" (John 14:2–3).

When we observe the Lord's Supper, we are reaffirming our faith, belief, and commitment that Jesus Christ is coming again (1 Cor. 11:26). Every time the baptismal waters are stirred and someone is baptized, those baptismal waters testify of a faith in the resurrection. The resurrection is that event which will take place at the coming of our Lord. The whole ministry of the church is geared toward the truth that Jesus Christ is coming again.

Jesus Is Coming for His Own

The Bible tells us that Jesus is coming for his own. "Now, dear brothers, I want you to know what happens to a Christian when he dies so that when it happens, you will not be full of sorrow, as those are who have no hope. For since we believe that Jesus died and then came back to life again, we can also believe that when Jesus returns, God will bring back with him all the Christians who have died. I can tell you this directly from the Lord: that we who are still living when the Lord returns will not rise to meet him ahead of those who are in their graves. For the Lord himself will come down from heaven with a mighty shout and with the soul-stirring cry of the archangel and the great trumpet-call of God. And the believers who are dead will be the first to rise to meet the Lord. Then we who are still alive and remain on the earth will be caught up with them in the clouds to meet the Lord in the air and remain with him forever. So comfort and encourage each other with this news" (1 Thess. 4:13–18, TLB).

"Everyone dies because all of us are related to Adam, being members of his sinful race, and wherever there is sin, death results. But all who are related to Christ will rise again. Each, however, in his own turn: Christ rose first; then when Christ comes back, all his people will come alive again. I tell you this, my brothers: an earthly body made of flesh and blood cannot get into God's kingdom. These perishable bodies of ours are not the right kind to live forever. But I am telling you this strange and wonderful secret: we shall not all die, but we shall all be given new bodies! It will all happen in a moment, in the twinkling of an eye, when the last trumpet is blown. For there will be a trumpet blast from the sky and all the Christians who have died will suddenly become alive, with new bodies that will never, never die; and then we who are still alive shall suddenly have new bodies too. For our earthly bodies, the ones we have now that can die, must be transformed into heavenly bodies that cannot perish but will live forever" (1 Cor. 15:22–23,50–53, TLB).

And in speaking of the time when the Lord shall snatch out of this earth those that are his, Matthew said: "Two men will be working together in the fields, and one will be taken, the other left. Two women will be going about their household tasks; one will be taken, the other left. So be prepared, for you don't know what day your Lord is coming" (Matt. 24:40–42, TLB). He is giving us a panoramic view of a grand reunion that someday will take place. The Lord will return for those who have been redeemed by his own precious blood. All of the good-byes of a thousand yesterdays will be blended into the glorious reunion of all the saints of all the ages.

What will happen? First, the dead in Christ will rise (1 Thess. 4:16). Then the living Christians will be caught up (1 Thess. 4:17). At this time, a great change will take place in us. Corruptible things cannot inherit incorruption (1 Cor. 15:50). These bodies that are subject to disease, limitations, and decay have to be changed, gloriously transformed, made eternal, made immortal. We do not know what that change will be, but we know that "it doth not yet appear what we shall be: but we know that, when he shall appear, we shall be like him; for we shall see him as he is" (1 John 3:2).

When the church is caught up and taken out of the earth, then a period of great tribulation will take place on the earth. Paul said about the Antichrist: "The mystery of iniquity doth already work: only he who now letteth will let, until he be taken out of the way. And then shall that Wicked be revealed, whom the Lord shall consume with the spirit of his mouth, and shall destroy with the brightness of his coming" (2 Thess. 2:7–8).

The Holy Spirit is the one who permits. When the Holy Spirit is taken away, the restraint will be gone. Then the tribulation will come. And the promise of God to us is that he will never leave us. The Holy Spirit cannot leave without taking us with him. We shall be saved from the wrath that is going to take place. "For God hath not appointed us to wrath" (1 Thess. 5:9). The tribulation period throughout the Word of God is indicated as a time of wrath. It is a time of judgment. The Christians will not have to endure the judgment of God upon this earth. So the saints will be taken out. A great change will take place, and the tribulation will come upon the earth. Jesus is coming for his own.

Jesus Is Coming with His Own

Following that time he will come with his saints. This time he will come back to the earth to establish his kingdom, his reign. "I saw thrones, and they sat upon them, and judgment was given unto them: and I saw the souls of them that were beheaded for the witness of Jesus, and for the Word of God, and which had not worshipped the beast, neither his image, neither had received his mark upon their foreheads, or in their hands; and they lived and reigned with Christ a thousand years. But the rest of the dead lived not again until the thousand years were finished. This is the first resurrection. Blessed and holy is he that hath part in the first resurrection: on such the second death hath not power, but they shall be priests of God and of Christ, and shall reign with him a thousand years" (Rev. 20:4–6).

"Behold, the Lord cometh with ten thousands of his saints

To execute judgment upon all" (Jude 14–15). A time is coming when Jesus will come with us. We shall rise to meet him; then he shall come to the earth to establish his reign.

That means two things. First, it means a literal reign upon the earth. He is going to establish a kingdom. He is the King of kings, and there cannot be a king without a kingdom. The kingdom will last a thousand years upon this earth before the resurrection of the lost and before the final judgment upon Satan. Some feel the word *thousand* is symbolic. It is mentioned six times in the book of Revelation, and it always refers to a specific time period. There is no reason for us to think that it does not refer to a specific time period here.

He will establish a literal reign upon the earth. "Unto us a child is born, unto us a son is given: and the government shall be upon his shoulder: and his name shall be called Wonderful, Counsellor, The mighty God, The everlasting Father, The Prince of Peace. Of the increase of his government and peace there shall be no end, upon the throne of David, and upon his kingdom, to order it, and to establish it with judgment and with justice from henceforth even for ever" (Isa. 9:6–7). That has not happened yet. He is not reigning in an eternal kingdom upon this earth right now. Yet a kingdom with judgment and justice will be established. Christ has not yet been crowned King of kings and Lord of lords upon this earth.

The fulfillment of the promise that "every knee should bow . . . every tongue should confess" (Phil. 2:10–11) has not occurred yet. When the angel talked to Mary about the man that would be born to her, the angel said to her: "He shall be great, and shall be called the Son of the Highest: and the Lord God shall give unto him the throne of his father David: And he shall reign over the house of Jacob for ever; and of his kingdom there shall be no end" (Luke 1:32–33). That hasn't happened yet. So Jesus is going to come *for* his saints and then will return with his saints to establish his literal reign upon the earth.

We are going to reign with him. He "hath made us kings and priests unto God and his Father" (Rev. 1:6). "If we suffer, we shall also reign with him" (2 Tim. 2:12). The saints are going to be given their proper place in this world. We are living in a world that laughts at the godly, spurns right, and elevates wrong. But there is coming a day when Jesus Christ will return, and we shall reign and rule with him.

Jesus Is Coming Soon

Jesus is coming soon.

"But as the days of Noe were, so shall also the coming of the Son of man be. For as in the days that were before the flood they were eating and drinking, marrying and giving in marriage, until the day that Noe entered into the ark, And knew not until the flood came, and took them all away; so shall also the coming of the Son of man be" (Matt. 24:37–39).

"Likewise also as it was in the days of Lot; they did eat, they drank, they bought, they sold, they planted, they builded; But the same day that Lot went out of Sodom it rained fire and brimstone . . . and destroyed them all. Even thus shall it be in the day when the Son of man is revealed" (Luke 17:28–30).

"This know also, that in the last days perilous times shall come. For men shall be lovers of their own selves, covetous, boasters, proud, blasphemers, disobedient to parents, unthankful, unholy, Without natural affection, trucebreakers, false accusers, incontinent, fierce, despisers of those that are good, Traitors, heady, highminded, lovers of pleasures more than lovers of God; Having a form of godliness, but denying the power thereof; from such turn away" (2 Tim. 3:1–5).

"But of the times and the seasons, brethren, ye have no need that I write unto you. For yourselves know perfectly that the day of the Lord so cometh as a thief in the night. For when they shall say, Peace and safety; then sudden destruction cometh upon them, as travail upon a woman with child; and they shall not escape. But ye, brethren, are not in darkness, that that day should overtake you as a thief. Ye are all the children of light, and the children of the day: we are not of the night, nor of darkness. Therefore let us not sleep, as do others; but let us watch and be sober" (1 Thess. 5:1–6).

When is he coming? One thing is for sure: Nobody knows. When we say Jesus is coming soon, we are declaring what the Word of God teaches. Any Christian who does not live his Christian experience in the anticipation of the return of Jesus Christ will live a defeated life. There will be no urgency about our witness. If we view life as simply threescore and ten and a grave at the end, we will not be too serious about serving God now. We will never become too serious about being good stewards of our possessions, time, and talents. We will never be concerned that we reach the lost or that we involve ourselves with missions around the world because we have no sense of urgency of the return of Christ.

From the first Christian generation there was the admonition, "Be ready. Be looking for his return. Be anticipating his coming. You do not know when he is coming." All of the signs point to the return. We can read in history about Sodom and Gomorrah and the days preceding the flood. It is apparent that our world is as wicked today as any day in history. Our society is moving toward a time of absolute rebellion against God. The Bible tells us that in the last days this will be the pattern.

He is coming soon. That is why we labor. That is why we serve God. That is why there is a sense of urgency about the work that God has committed to us.

Jesus declared that he would return when men were not expecting him. So any time we say, "He can't come," that is the prime time when he may come. I do not understand all the signs or details. That is unimportant. God did not put us on his program committee. He put us on his preparation committee. He is going to do what he pleases to do. He is going to come when it pleases him to come. Our task is to be ready.

Are there things in our lives that would make us unprepared to greet our returning Lord? We should not want to become simply students of all of the prophecy about the coming of Christ. We should desire to become practitioners of the disciplines of the Christian faith that will prepare us for his coming.

BROADMAN